40+ AND *Fabulous*

40+ AND
Fabulous

Moving Forward
Fierce, Focused,
and Full of Life!

SONDRA WRIGHT

*Bella*HOUSE
PUBLISHING
North Carolina

40+ and Fabulous
Moving Forward Fierce, Focused, and Full of Life!

ISBN 978-0-9831265-6-0

Library of Congress Control Number: 2010918073

Manufactured in the United States of America

BellaHouse Publishing
P. O. Box 36355
Greensboro, NC 27416-6355
www.bellahousepub.com

Website
www.40plusandfabulous.com

CONTENTS

ACKNOWLEDGEMENTS...ix

FOREWORD xi

INTRODUCTION xv

Jane Ganahl..1

Darlene Bauer..7

Eileen Fulton 11

Elline Surianello... 17

Norma Hollis.. 23

Terry Kohl.. 27

Dr Johnetta Cole.. 33

Kim Cameron 37

Tanya Hutchinson 45

Roselle Wilson 51

Kim Harris.. 57

Brenda Pollard 63

AJ.. 69

Nancy Cranbourne 75

Yana Berlin... 79

Eva LaRue 87

Sue Taylor 91

Joanne and Barbara.. 97

Connie Vasquez 101

Loretta Petit 107

Catherine Hickland 113

Acharya Sri Khadi Madama 119

Tina Stull... 125

Judie Bucholz 131

Yolanda Carr. 137

Andrea Vanessa Wright 143

Minnie Forte-Brown. 149

STRAIGHT TALK AND MEN'S THOUGHTS
ON 40+ and FABULOUS WOMEN 155

Frank 157

Dave 159

Pablo 161

Frank 163

Jimmy. 165

Eric 167

Jeffrey 169

Bruce 171

Derrick. 173

Ryan 175

Trey 177

George 179

Darrell 181

"AH-HAH" COLLECTION. 185

AFTERWORD. 191

ABOUT THE AUTHOR 193

CONTRIBUTORS' DIRECTORY 195

DEDICATION

To my niece, Barrington:
When I first laid eyes on you—you took my breath away.
From that moment, all I've wanted
is to make this world a better place for you to grow up
and grow old in. You are the future,
Forty Plus and Fabulous!

ACKNOWLEDGEMENTS

Write a book! Who? Me? I don't know anything about writing a book.

First, let me say this book would not have been possible if not for the generosity of the contributing women, who opened up their hearts to me and the world. To them I say a humble thank you.

Additionally, I must say a special thank you to the contributing men who think women over forty rock, and were an absolute joy to work with.

Thanks to the mega talented and ultra patient, Kim Harris, who took what was an ill-formatted, color-coded, may have, or not have been a manuscript, saw what I could not see, and helped create a masterpiece. You are the best!

Juanita Dix, for a fleeting moment you were concerned that you weren't going to be able to nail this book cover design, but you did. Your work is everything I wanted and more.

Tiona Honey, your assistance in transcribing interviews was priceless. Your reminding me that this book was my baby and I must give birth to it was beyond priceless. Thank you.

Lucinda Cross, thank you for stirring up the gift and awakening the book that was asleep within me.

The dynamic duo of Nancey Flowers; for guiding and being there to answer my questions along the way and Patricia Harris; for your invaluable suggestions, commitment to excellence and letting me know when it was time to let go.

To my sister-friend Brenda Pollard, it must have been about 20 years ago on a night when I was visiting you in Memphis that we made a pact to stay healthy, active, young at heart and age appropriate sexy. That was the night my dear friend, a seed was planted and took root.

To my dream team; Toni Davis, Gerry Shoffner, Cynthia Sharpe, Jean Waters, Marilyn Watts, and Sandra Wright-Wallington. From the moment I shared this idea with you, your enthusiasm and confidence in me has helped me keep hope alive. Thank you for believing in me.

To the two most fabulous forty plus inspirations in my life; my mother, Ruth Briggs, who looks at me and sees a woman who can do anything, and my mother-in-law, Rozenia Wright, who at 87 years of age embodies all the charm, grace, poise and sophistication I hope to someday possess. Thank you both for praying for me during times when I didn't have the strength to pray for myself.

To my dad, John; brother and sister, Pernell and Angie; sister-in-law, Treavesa; and, my beautiful niece, Barrington. Your belief, prayers, love, and support mean everything to me and truly is the wind beneath my wings.

This simply could not have been possible without the faithful support of the most wonderful husband in the universe. John, when I wanted to give up babe, you refused to let my dream die, and I thank you for that and love you more than words can say.

And Father God, most of all I thank you. When I asked, *"Who am I and what do I have to offer in a book,"* during the quiet stillness of night, you whispered to me... *"You are Forty Plus and Fabulous."* From there, you gave me everything I would need to get it done.

FOREWORD

We all know how the adage goes: *"When you're young you want to be older, and when you're older you want to be young again."* Many of us can identify with this, right? We spent a great deal of time in our youth in a race towards the golden finish—turning 18. We then spent another three years eagerly anticipating the pièce de résistance, turning 21. We couldn't wait until we were legal... legal to drink, legal to drive and legal and able to have the means to move out of our parents homes, make our own decisions and live the lives we wanted to live. Yes, this sense of urgency was present in all of us because as teenagers who were desperate for a modicum of power and the ability to finally control our own lives, age translated to independence and oh, how we so wanted to be free!

And then, for a great deal of us, the shift happens. While some of us moved happily along in our lives, eagerly adding each successive age to our birth tally and proudly wearing our age on our sleeves, others are gripped by an overwhelming fear. And it is this fear that seizes the lives of those who, after the age of 21, fear what age and getting older means for their lives, loves and careers. They allow themselves to buy into the myth that aging is a bad thing, and tend to waste a great deal of time refusing to acknowledge it, while desperately trying everything possible to reverse it. And it is this mindset that is so apparent in our culture today.

So many in our society are investing huge amounts of time and money, lifting, tucking, botoxing and lying about their age; fighting hard against that one thing we were born to do...get older. And what they learn, when they finally give themselves a chance to embrace it, is that age is their calling card to a world yet explored. That it is not so much about getting older than it is about growing bolder and that there is an entire world out there awaiting them—all they have to do is have the audacity to believe it!

Growing older really is about *"Moving forward fierce, focused and full of life."* In her debut book, *40+ and Fabulous*, Sondra Wright is showing us how to live this quote to the fullest. Sondra has brought us stories of empowerment and boldness from women of differing ages and various backgrounds. Many of these women are in the public eye, and have embraced their age in a way that speaks to a life of exclusivity. A life that one would be and should be jealous of if they were not actually given the chance at the same opportunity. But thankfully, growing older is an equal opportunity for all, and no one has to be left behind unless they choose to do so.

As I write these words, I am sitting on the precipice of my golden birthday—the big 4-0 and I cannot wait. My own journey to forty has been marked with changing my age for the benefit of others. Although mine was more about me adding years to my age frame and appearing older than what I was. I would say I was 30 when I was only 27...or that I was nearly 35 when I'd just turned 32. I have an extremely young looking face, which is both a blessing and a curse, and I believed I needed the accumulation of years to add credibility to my life and experiences. And now with the golden age of 40 quickly approaching I feel as if I've arrived and no longer need a false sense of security to do what age and the wisdom of years can provide and will do for me naturally. So exciting... so exciting! Life really does begin at 40 and with Sondra's words and research I can embrace this time in my life feeling nothing short of fabulous! And you can too!

Allow this book to teach you how to stand toe-to-toe with the cultural giants of our time who are painting a picture of death and doom after 40. Adopt the mindset of the women interviewed in this book, so that you can profess to yourself and the world, *"I am not getting older, I am getting bolder, and there is nothing the world can do to stop me!"* Sondra has set out on a personal journey to change the mentality of women around the world, reminding them of what it truly means to age gracefully. Teaching them through the example of herself and others that acknowledging who you

FOREWORD

are at your core means embracing all facets of your life, and standing in a truth that no one else can claim. And, that age brings with it a fierceness and boldness that really is wasted on the young.

So, embrace your age, create your own fountain of youth, and be bold enough to stand in the face of a society that would demand that you need to be younger in order to be relevant, and show them the true beauty of who you are, age and all. Demand the best of your life and never allow anything, especially your age, to stop you from living your dreams. Because as I stated earlier, your life is waiting for you... you just have to have the audacity to believe it!

Tonoa Bond, *The Audacity Expert*
Coach, Author, Speaker,
Educator in Human Behavior

INTRODUCTION

I was sitting down one day as a young girl in the mid 70's trying to calculate how old I would be in the year 2000. At the time, 36 seemed so old and I remember thinking I would probably be dead by then. But here I am, 2010, alive, kicking and loving every minute of it; the good, bad and everything in between!

When I first embarked upon this project, I had no idea how incredibly important it would be. For me, aging has not been an issue. I promised myself a long time ago that I would age well and go gracefully into the process. As far as I'm concerned, and that's all that really matters, I look pretty darned good for my age. I hate exercise. Other than that I've taken reasonably good care of myself.

My secret desire is at eighty years old to be featured as a timeless beauty in Essence Magazine. Turning forty was not a crisis point in my life and I look forward to, with great anticipation, fifty, sixty and every decade beyond. As I was gathering stories for my book, I received an email from a young woman one day that really impressed upon me the importance of women having role models and positive images of women living and loving life at forty and beyond. Her email read as follows:

"Hey, Sondra!

I'm 38, soon to be 39. I don't have any advice for you, but I'd LOVE to know where you published the article. I could use the encouragement. I'm actually kind of upset about turning 40. Not sure what my deal is. 40 just seems...old. Fortunately, I look a lot younger than I am, and hence, my age is a super-high-security secret. My work is in freelance writing and the internet area, and my picture is everywhere online. Ageism is rampant in the internet space, just like entertainment. I'm afraid people won't think I'm as current, if I'm over 40.

I know I sound ridiculous, but there it is.

So please let me know when and where your article is published! Thanks!"

Of course I went online and looked her up. The girl didn't lie...she looks nowhere near her age. Sadly what she doesn't know is us over forty divas would not trade places with her if you offered us two Brad Pitts, a Will Smith and a Denzel. Well at least she didn't know it before now!

When I was in my mid twenties, I remember shopping one day for a greeting card in Phar-Mor. You might remember the discount drug store with the cheesy slogan, *"Phar-Mor power buying gives you Phar-Mor buying power."* Hey, it worked! Anyway, while scanning the greeting card section, suddenly and quite unexpectedly; this loud fart goes off in the aisle. My head snapped around, a reflex reaction, and since there were only two of us in the aisle I was able to quickly assess that the gaseous explosion had erupted from the elder lady reading the greeting cards behind me. She was completely unfazed by the incident. She did not look to the left, she did not look to the right, nor did she offer up any apologies. And I remember thinking how awesome it was going to be to grow old and just fart wherever and whenever I wanted!

One of the most liberating quotes I have ever read was written by noted psychiatrist and psychotherapist, Fritz Perls, *"I do my own thing and you do your thing. I am not in this world to live up to your expectations, and you are not in this world to live up to mine. You are you and I am I."*

After 40, my likeability score went off the radar. That was because I finally got it; and once I got it, I was free. I could just be me and not have to prove myself worthy or acceptable to anyone else. I accepted the fact that not everyone is going to like or agree with me and I became very careful about whom I allowed in my personal space. After all, I'm the Queen! And girls, until you recognize yourselves for the queens you are, you will give your power to anyone with a pulse; draining and sapping you, until you lose the will to live. People can be such energy vampires. Knowing who to give credence to and who to ignore is a beautiful thing.

INTRODUCTION

I heard Joel Osteen say one day, *"Twenty-five percent of the people you meet won't like you and never will. Twenty-five percent won't like you, but can be persuaded to. Twenty-five percent will like you, but could be persuaded not to. And, twenty-five percent will like you, and stand by you no matter what. Life gets a lot freer when you realize, if this person doesn't like me, if they don't want to be my friend, if they don't want to give me the time of day - it's no big deal. Do not waste your valuable time and energy playing up to them; trying to change their mind; trying to convince them that you're important."* How freeing is that?

It's great to be in a position to make your own decisions without any outside influence or pressure; just do what you want and what your inner voice is guiding you to do. I haven't always been in tune with that part of myself (you may call it your Higher Power, Spirit, Source, Flow, etc.). In fact, I spent the majority of my younger years ignoring the instructions of my God voice. I married for the first time at age twenty-three. My mom was mortified. In fact, when my husband-to-be at the time, phoned my parents to tell them of our intent to marry, they laughed at him. I still get chills when I recall the gurgling, gasping sound that rose up from my mother's throat, when she called me to confirm the impending marriage as true. *"Why?"* she asked me. And I, in all the infinite wisdom I could have possessed as a twenty-three year old replied, *"Because two can live cheaper than one."*

It was a Justice of the Peace wedding, and my parents did not attend. I can recall my fiancée driving us to the courthouse, with my brother and my brother's roommate in the backseat. When we stopped for gas I heard my inner voice screaming for me to jump out of the car and run as fast as my legs would carry me. *"Run girl!" "Run!" "Jump-out-of-the-car–and-RUN!"* Some of you reading this know exactly what I'm talking about because you heard the exact same thing and you ignored it too. But we learned from those mistakes and we became better because of them, didn't we?

Finally, after years of trial and error, doing it my way and getting it wrong most of the time, I am completely and totally dependent. I ask the Lord about EVERYTHING! I'm like the needy girlfriend you had back in the day. You remember her name. She was the one who brought all of her issues to you and phoned incessantly, all hours of the day and night. You felt like the two of you were joined at the hip because she didn't make a move without you. If there was some place she wanted to go, she always checked to see if you were going. If you weren't going, no matter how badly she wanted to, she didn't go either. THAT'S ME! And there's no shame in my game. As a matter of fact, I'm asking Him right now to write this book because I have no idea what I'm doing.

I just celebrated my 46th birthday this year and, as you know from reading a little earlier in the chapter, I'm pretty anti-exercise. I stand very firm in my belief that the only thing that should lead to perspiration and heavy breathing is sex. Nonetheless, I'm still determined to look good. I just need to do so on my terms, and in a way that's comfortable for me. I had considered Pilates off and on for about two years, but was afraid it was yet something else I wouldn't stick with. Memories of the unused treadmills, steppers, hip and thigh machines and gym memberships that had become my reality always flooded my mind.

Finally, I decided *"What the heck? I might as well add one more thing to the collection."* I called a couple of Pilates studios and happened upon one that was just starting a beginners midday class. This is where I met Tonya Martin of Get Fit Pilates Studio, and she began to transform my body and my life.

In the many, many roles we play as women, it's easy for our attention to be all over the place. Pilates will challenge your body, but it can be difficult to do the routines if your mind is wandering, so it sort of forces you to be in the moment. This was great for me because my mind is completely engaged; not on the bills that have to be paid, the dishes in the sink, or my next client appointment. Except for the occasional daydream about a Banana Royale from Baskin-Robbins, I am completely in the moment. Pilates renews me, clears my mind and the results are incredible. My hips are more toned and I had no idea my butt had dropped until Pilates lifted it back up again. It was here that I also learned the importance of doing Kegel exercises to strengthen the muscles of my pelvic floor.

Now, don't miss this one, ladies! Weak pelvic floor muscles can cause you to have a leaky bottom; number one and/or number two. There are several factors that can attribute to the breakdown of those muscles; like pregnancy, childbirth, caesarean section, aging and excess weight, but the good news is, and thank God there is good news, a very nice man named Dr. Arnold Kegel, a gynecologist, developed some exercise techniques for strengthening the pelvic floor. Now, I'm not exactly sure what Dr.Kegel's motives were here, especially since the exercises can also make the vagina tighter... hmmm. But hey, if it's going to help me maintain control over my bodily functions, then this is one of those cases where the risk—just might be worth the reward.

Something that has undeniably changed since coming into my forties is my vision. I've never needed corrective lenses, but I've noticed, over time, it has become increasingly difficult for me to focus in on small text, except when I'm outdoors in natural sunlight. A couple of years ago I went to the eye doctor, all but begging for glasses. I am not in denial, okay? I am fully prepared to expect some normal age-related vision changes and, truth be told, I think glasses are sexy and make the wearer look quite stylish and sophisticated. I was already picking out my Dolce & Gabana frames, when the trusted professional came waltzing back in and informed me that my vision is still 20/20. He said that I was just suffering a little dry eye; a side effect of working long periods on the computer without blinking. I'm thinking, *"What kind of mess...?! You mean to tell me I'm not about to leave here with my sexy, sophisticated frames?"* I was so insistent, that he decided to test me again; this time for vision and glaucoma. When it was all said and done, I was ushered to the door with some eye drops, the bill and a recommendation for some +1.00 reading glasses, *"if"* I wanted them. And there I stood—like a hypochondriac, wearing those crazy, dark, post eye exam glasses.

That was a couple of years ago, and today I've noticed I'm beginning to squint. Squinting is not good. Squinting is one of those movements responsible for the fine lines, or crows feet, that develop on the outside corner of the eye. So Doc, you may have won round one, but I'm coming back, and this time, I'm not leaving without my frames.

When it comes to taking care of me I believe in being proactive. I have a huge passion for natural and alternative wellness and speak to audiences weekly about this very topic. Ladies, let me share two important pieces of advice; first, stop waiting until you get sick, and start taking steps to prevent sickness in the first place. Second, stop investing more money on your weaves, mani-pedi's, and knock-off designer hand-bags, than you do on your health. They say that death and taxes are the only two certainties in life, but here's a third thing I can guarantee - a pretty corpse has zero value. I discovered the fountain of youth in the Gano Excel™ product line. Gourmet coffee, tea, hot chocolate and personal care products, all enriched with healthy, organic Ganoderma Lucidum. Yeah, I know, I couldn't pronounce it either. But I'm telling you, this is the most nutritious stuff on the planet. It restores your body to a natural state of good health and just makes you feel vibrant, youthful, strong, confident and sexy; make that very sexy, if you're drinking their Tongkat Ali. You can get more information on Gano Excel™ as well as a listing of my other favorite products, by visiting the "favorite things" directory on my website. And a special thank you to Dr. Marilyn Watts, for teaching me the benefits and the pronunciation of Ganoderma Lucidum.

Now while we're on the subject of taking care of ourselves, is it true that 80% of women are dissatisfied with their appearance? No one ever asked me but, if they had, I would have echoed the words of Mary J. Blige, *"I like what I see when I'm looking at me when I'm walking past the mirror!"*

As a matter of fact, all three of my mother's children have a love affair with our reflections in the mirror. I think we get it from my daddy. Listen ladies, at a certain age, you have to agree to either come to terms with it, or do something about it. I'm a 32B with skinny, flat feet, so no matter what way you flip me, the view is always flat, well...except maybe from the rear. My paternal grandmother, Sarah Staton, was a full figured woman with large breasts. I clearly remember her bras having reinforced panels on the front and about 5 hooks in the back. Because people were always telling me how much I looked like Sarah, you have to imagine for a moment through a child's eyes, the fear I felt at the thought of growing up, and **all** of me looking like Sarah!

By contrast, my mother is a very petite woman, stands 4'10," weighs 100 lbs and has no boobies at all. A flat chest would be her gift to me. I never minded really. In fact, one Mother's Day, several years ago, after I had married for the second time and now had 3 step children in my life; a stepdaughter from my first marriage and my current husband's two

INTRODUCTION

children from his first marriage, I wrote my mother a poem of thanks, expressing my gratitude for many things, including the small breasts that she had so selflessly bestowed upon me. She is going to kill me, but here is the poem for your reading pleasure...

> "Ma,
>
> Growing up, I took everything you did for granted. I just assumed you were being a mother, doing what mothers do. Now that I am grown and have three children, a grandchild, and a cat of my own, I realize nothing could be farther from the truth. I now know mothers are as unique as snowflakes. I now know my mother, though short in stature, was head and shoulders above the rest.
>
> This mother's day, I wanted to say "Thank You!"
>
> For all the diapers you changed, all the noses you wiped, all the colds you worried over, Thank You
>
> For making me the only fifth grader to wear a girdle, so I wouldn't be sway backed all my life, Thank You
>
> For perms and curls and making the best prom dress in the world, Thank You
>
> For all the times you let me sneak out of bed after Pernell and Angie had fallen asleep and for all the times you said "No," Thank You
>
> For the home made snow cream which, by the way, I never liked, Thank You
>
> For these itty, bitty, titties I hated when I was younger, but love now because they still stand proud when I take my bra off, Thank You!
>
> For making me clean the house every Saturday morning and the trips to the mall that followed, where you taught me the fine art of free cheese tastings at the Swiss Colony, Thank You
>
> For teaching me self-respect, Thank You
>
> For sharing your special T-bone steak, smothered in sautéed onions, mushrooms, and cheese, that you prepared when you thought no one else was around, Thank You

For PTA's and attending school plays, Thank You

For all the times you went without, so I wouldn't have to, Thank You

For mending shirts and socks and broken hearts, Thank You

For restraining yourself from knocking me out all the times I thought I was smarter than you, Thank You

For showing kindness to whomever I dated, or married, even when you disliked them, Thank You

For giving me a fine example of what a woman and a mother should be, Thank You."

See, as young women, we don't place enough value on our mothers and we certainly don't give them credit for knowing anything expect how to put food on the table and clean up after us, and even those acts of love we take for granted. But the truth is, my mother is the greatest woman I have ever known. I was twenty-six years old and going through a divorce when I realized she had been right about everything; men, sex, school, friendships—all of it. She is my original *Forty Plus and Fabulous* queen whom without I would be lost.

Alright, alright, that's enough about me. Let's talk about what to expect in this book.

I conducted several one-on-one interviews, and asked women from all walks of life what made being over forty the absolute best time of their lives. They were asked to share their lessons, hurdles, challenges, obstacles, secrets, habits and revelations with you. And did they ever!

I then asked men of all ages to tell me what they found most interesting, exciting, appealing and attractive about women in their forties and beyond. Let me tell you, the men were great! I received some good responses, some interesting responses, and some absolutely knock your socks off responses and I will leave it up to you to decide which is which.

Finally, there were so many brilliant interviews given, that this book could not contain them all. So to honor all of those whose stories did not make the final edit, I have assembled a compilation of their most memorable quotes. I call them my *"Ah-ha"* collection.

INTRODUCTION

I can't say enough about all the wonderful ladies, and men, who contributed to this book; who opened their hearts and shared their souls. In the beginning, I simply thought I was gathering information. And then, something completely wonderful and unexpected happened. Each of these ladies deposited a small miracle into my life; a nugget of wisdom that would set me on a course of change forever. These women made me laugh, made me cry, made me jump for joy and made me love me all the more. They each taught me a different lesson and I took away something very personal from each of their stories. Each of their stories is told in their own words. My hope is that they inspire you as much as they have inspired me. Note that while some stories may move you in exceptionally powerful ways, others may not. Each of you is unique and what you will get from each story is as individual as you are. But in the end, you should be filled with joy and expectation about where you are and where you're heading.

At the end of each of chapter, I have left a space for you to write your nugget of wisdom, and set your own personal course for change. Enjoy!

Sondra

JANE GANAHL

Author, *Naked on the Page: The Misadventures of My Unmarried Midlife.*
Former *San Francisco Chronicle* columnist,
Single Minded
Age 56

It's great to be over 40. With kids grown, you can completely reinvent yourself! After 45, I founded a literary festival, a monthly salon dinner for artists in San Francisco, became a Sunday newspaper columnist, edited one book and wrote another. Before that, I had been a struggling single mom and a grunt reporter. Other reasons it's great to be over 40; the biological clock that was ticking so loudly in your 30's grows quiet, and single women are free to date for all the right reasons—fun, sex, and friendship! Also, our women friendships grow deeper and more meaningful, and we learn the joys of true independence.

I've heard many times from men, not all unfortunately, but the men who are more spiritual or more evolved, that what really makes a woman beautiful, and what they are really drawn to is her confidence and sense of self, more so than her completely smooth and unwrinkled face.

I view women entirely different now than I did in my 20's. I think I was always very competitive with my fellow female counterparts, even with my friends. I don't think I saw it that way at the time. I felt like I always had to be the coolest or the prettiest and now, I think one of the blessings of getting older is that it sort of levels the playing field, and we can really look at each other as humans. When you take away the competitiveness, you can really have some very deep and meaningful relationships.

People often ask what are the pros and cons of dating over 40. For me, the good news is you know who you are. You know what you are looking for and what you're not as opposed to when you are in your, 20's or 30's just dating and trying to figure that out. But once you do figure it out, the bad news is there are fewer people that you are willing to hang out with, and the dating pool is smaller. But I don't mind that. I'd much rather have fewer dates with someone who is more connected to me, than trying to fit square pegs in round holes, which I did my entire life.

If you really love yourself, and you work on being your best person—and I don't mean being your richest and best looking, but your best, most evolved spiritual self—that will draw men to you. The flip side is to work on yourself so that you don't worry about finding a man so much. Work on yourself so that your life is full, so that you have good relationships with your family or your friends or whomever, and find some personal meaning in your life. It seems to me that people who have meaning in their lives are less rigid about thinking that marriage has to happen or their life will be over. Don't for a minute think that getting married is going to solve your problems. It can actually create problems that are much worse.

Finding meaningful relationships is most important, as well as finding meaning in your everyday life—in your work and extracurricular pursuits. This is the key to a happy and fulfilled life. I know people who may not be as happy with their 9 to 5 jobs. They are slaving away at their day jobs but have extra-curricular activities, like volunteering, that really float their boats and make them feel like they are contributing something. And at the end of the day, success is feeling like you really enjoyed yourself doing whatever it was that you were doing. It was either fun, meaningful, or both. It means you found your true calling and to me, that's real success. It wasn't until I became a writer that I could go home at the end of the day not feeling like I had been drained or stressed out.

That whatever it was that I was doing was giving back to me instead of just taking and taking and taking. That was the first time I really felt successful; sort of working in harmony with what it was I thought that I was on the planet to do.

About ten years ago, I became aware of hormonal changes. I've been thin my whole life and my sister is rubenesque. As a young woman, I remember always wishing I had more curves, and she always wishing that she were thinner. Here I was gaining weight like crazy. It was a couple of years ago that I discovered Zumba, a Latin cardio dance. It's easy on my knees and ankles and definitely meets my needs for exercise. I hope to do it forever. I also go to an herbalist because I'm in San Francisco and you have to do those kinds of things here. I'm kidding, of course, but I am a big believer in alternative medicine. I

"WHEN THINGS ARE REMOVED FROM YOU, YOU CAN EITHER FEEL SORRY FOR YOURSELF OR USE THEM AS CUES TO REINVENT YOURSELF."

think that's been enormously helpful in keeping my health in balance because I go 90 miles an hour every single day. I've seen women who are in their 70's, who really take good care of themselves; they eat healthy, their hair is this gorgeous gray and they're just so sexy to me. They really look like they've got it going on because they're healthy, and just seem to have great self-esteem.

I'm a very social being, and I always come away from spending time with people I care about feeling such a profound sense of well-being. My dad is still alive and my daughter is now 30 so she and I are like best friends. These are things I do that are not just options but necessities. If left to my own devices, I could be at my computer working from 7 in the morning until 8 at night, and I know that's bad for me. I make myself take breaks to take care of my house, to exercise and to spend time with people and my pets, too, to have something warm and fuzzy to hold and cuddle. For me, that connection to life is the key.

I was in my early 40's when my daughter went to college in Maine. She was about as far away as one can get. I was suddenly a single woman. Then my mother died and afterwards, my sister died. All of this happened within a year. It was sort of sink or swim at that point. I was so devastated. My life had been forcibly changed and I thought, "So what do I do?" I asked for a lot of help spiritually and I started a literary festival in San Francisco. That literary festival is now ten years old and booming. We had 450 authors attend over a period of 9 days last year. That was the most profound thing about my 40's, discovering my possibilities once I stopped defining myself in limited ways. I had been a working single mom and then my daughter went away. I had been a daughter to a woman I loved very much who also went away.

When things are removed from you, you can either feel sorry for yourself or use them as cues to reinvent yourself. That's what I did. It took several years to feel like it was a successful process but it was enormously successful. I'm a big advocate for women who feel like they hit 40 and think things go down-hill from that point.

I tell them to look around and think of other things that they might like to do, because there is never a better time to strike out in a new direction than in your 40's. I think that it's just the perfect time.

For some women, it happens when they put on that cool new dress and strut their stuff down the street, feeling beautiful and confident. But for me, these days it's really about my work and the stuff that I do. Whether I'm reading from my book or doing an event around something I've written, when I'm standing up at the podium or when I'm writing at my computer and I'm feeling like, *"Oh my gosh, this is really clicking."*

Because my book is personal and it is about my life, I just feel like I am shining. I'm in my element. The messages in my book are kind of encouraging and upbeat for women. It must be how a minister feels up in the pulpit. I'm far from being a minister but my book does have a sort of evangelistic feel to it. It's what I do well. I'm 56 now. I no longer feel like I turn heads like I used to in my youth, so I sort of interpret the word "beautiful" as feeling fabulous, and these are the things that make me feel most fabulous. However, I do feel very sexy when someone is drawn to me because of who I am and what I do; when I'm appearing for a reading and a guy comes up to me because he's drawn to my confidence. That's when I feel that I can really vamp out.

So, keep a good attitude about your 40's. It really can be the beginning of the absolute best years of your life. That is not simply a cliché; it's absolutely true. It's all about attitude and it's all about thinking expansively. The best is yet to come!

WHAT GOLDEN NUGGETS DID YOU GET FROM THIS TREASURE CHEST OF WISDOM?

DARLENE BAUER

Retired English Teacher, Former Consultant for Houghton Mifflin

Age 73

Just a few days ago, I told someone that I didn't know why we are so "youth-oriented," because I just turned 73 and life has never been happier, healthier, more exciting and fulfilling.

My current joy in life is actually a result of jogging along a life path with my nose to the grindstone while learning from my mistakes, continuing to study, keeping physically active and socially engaged, and developing an ever-expanding spiritual awareness.

My mom kept me. She tried to abort me five times and that's okay. I don't believe that any woman should try and have a baby that she is not prepared for, but I was meant to be here. I was born on Christmas Eve, in a Salvation Army Hospital in Chicago. She was a wonderful mother and a difficult mother. She married a factory worker who adopted me and loved me. Daddy Dietz was the world's best bear hugger.

I didn't know until I was age 42 that I had been born hard of hearing. They taught reading in small circles so I became a compulsive reader. I also read lips and body language. I pretty much know when a politician is lying. In spite of that handicap and really poor grades I managed to finish college and then earn a master's degree.

Since my family were devout atheists I was always curious about what the rest of the world was doing—praying, ringing bells, etc. So I explored religions and other cultures.

My first husband was a Navy Jet Pilot. He could communicate with machines but not with people. My second husband turned out to be a con man. I made him so mad that he dropped dead on cue. His fourth wife

(I learned after his death that I was number six – at least), selected my current husband for me.

"IF IT DROOPS, WORK IT OUT OR FIX IT AND GO ON WITH LIFE."

After I divorced my first husband, I started studying abroad during summers: Worcester College, Oxford, Cambridge Summer School, a course of Art and Literature in Greece, and then, spent a summer studying Renaissance Art in Florence, Italy. I'm still taking classes at UCSD and Mira Costa College.

After retiring nine years ago from a thirty-two year career as an English teacher, I married my third husband Art, moved from Chula Vista, CA to Encinitas, CA and joined Art's involvement in an athletic group for senior citizens called "Get Off Your Rockers." Art had a nice social life established and since I enjoy cooking and entertaining, I fit right in.

Soon I began attending aqua exercise classes at the Magdalena Eke YMCA in Encinitas every morning and began my own circle of friends and acquaintances there. I also joined the American Association of University Women, Planned Parenthood and The Friends of Jung. Also, Art and I have taken many trips around the U.S. and abroad during our nine years of marriage.

Since I am very goal-oriented I was uneasy about not working. I took a job as a consultant with Houghton-Mifflin Book Company, back when California was working on their textbook adoption seven years ago. As a high school teacher, I had no clue about elementary school textbooks. But I learned and had a great time traveling to many schools and visiting teachers in San Diego County. That job lasted a year and a half.

Art and I have a great marriage. I had three daughters. My eldest daughter and I have been estranged for nine years. My second daughter, a bi-polar/schizophrenic, died of breast cancer seven years ago. My youngest daughter and I are best friends.

So I've spent much of my life studying abnormal psychology up close. I've lived through poverty and hard times, worked as a waitress, played the role of officer's wife, struck out on my own for 18 years, taught English as a second language to adults, taught high school English for 14 years, worked as a consultant for a text book company and have now completed writing my own book.

In May of 2005, I suffered through four days of discomfort with a bottom of the barrel house guest from hell and decided that there were no books that addressed this particular subject. So with the encouragement and help of many friends, my book, *Host or Hostage? A Guide for Surviving House Guests* is now ready to market.

I just created my own company, Barthur House Publishing, Inc., and I have been speaking to women's groups about the issues of entertaining houseguests. I use a PowerPoint presentation employing the 21 cartoons from my book.

How do I look? Well, I believe in using all the help I can get from dermatologists and plastic surgeons. We spend tons of money on cars but it's our own faces and figures we need to use and encounter in the mirror each day. If it droops, work it out or fix it and go on with life.

I love people and I believe that the best soul food is a smile. I can't seem to stop myself from speaking to everyone I meet and when possible, learn a few things about them. While I was doing research for this book I would ask anyone I met, anywhere, *"Have you ever had an interesting houseguest experience?"* People opened up. The anecdotal material in my book is often amazing.

Finding such great joy as an advanced senior citizen has been a long path fraught with pain, confusion, hard work and either luck or spiritual guidance from another realm.

But at 73, life is healthy, happy and GLORIOUS.

WHAT GOLDEN NUGGETS DID YOU GET FROM THIS TREASURE CHEST OF WISDOM?

_____

_____

_____

_____

_____

_____

_____

_____

_____

EILEEN FULTON

Actress, Daytime TV Series *As the World Turns*

Age 75

When I was a little girl, my mother had a group of friends; there was Dot and Hazel and another woman whom I can't remember, and I was so distressed because my mother was the youngest. As a child, it was always more fun to be older because in my small group of little friends, the older girl got to take charge—the oldest girl was the one responsible; so I felt so sorry for my mother being the "baby" of the group and I guess I've always felt that way.

I've embraced each new decade with expectancy. It must be that way. We keep hearing about and reading about "youth orientation." Poor children—don't know what it's all about unless they've gone through a lot. I think as you get older, you add experience, and with experience, every turn in your life should be for the better; that's my attitude. Just look at television—if you must. It's all about youth, youth and youth. I think youth is beautiful. It's like a new flower—a new budding—but it doesn't have the experience of an open rose or a beautiful full grown orchid. There's more to life than just youth. I think it's a wonderful thing, don't cut them short, but let's expand...let's live. I believe in living and enjoying. I find that very important.

From the inside out, what makes a woman beautiful is her outlook. There are some very beautiful people who are not very beautiful to me anymore. It's your whole approach. Health helps. Good health, taking good care of yourself, being proud of whoever you are, at whatever age you are. I've always been proud of that. I've always felt like *"Yeah, I'm experienced...I know things!"*

I hate mammograms. I always take a Xanax before I go in for one. You'd think they were going to chop my breast off or something. They say if they had to perform a similar procedure on a man, they would quickly invent another way to get it done. About 10 years ago I was reading a book I had picked up in the airport. I love to read, that's my passion. I had picked up a book by Danielle Steele because I could read half of it going to California and the other half coming back. It was called, *"Lightning"* and I thought, *"Oh good, we may get struck by lightning, so I'll read this."* Well, the lightning was the woman. She was a very busy woman; she hadn't gotten a mammogram in 7 years, and during this visit, her doctor said those fateful words, *"We need to talk."* At the time I was reading this book I hadn't had a mammogram in 7 years because I just dreaded it. I remember always thinking to myself, *"I'm fine."* It was a gruesome story and in reading it, you went through every process of the cancer. It was so awful that when I finished the book I didn't want to touch it anymore. I threw it in the trash and thought, *"I better go have myself checked!"* When I went, it was just like the pages of the book were unfolding when my doctor said, "Eileen, we need to talk." We did the procedure over and over again. It was a precancerous little thing that they removed and I thought, *"Thank God for Danielle Steele and that book!"*

I get enough rest and I keep my mind active. I am always learning music and doing concert work—that's one of the best things I can do for myself—and reading; I read all the time. I'm about to begin the biography of Mary Todd Lincoln, which I'm really looking forward to, and I just finished a fabulous book called, *A Country Called Home,* by Tim Barnes. And in a few months, I'll be looking forward to reading *Forty Plus and Fabulous.* I'm so glad you're doing this. It's so important. I used to receive fan mail from people that said *"Act your age!"* And I used to think, *"Well, what in the hell do you mean by that?!"*

Don't let people run you down just because you're over 40. That's stupid! Look at the European idea of the older woman. The woman who has mystery, who has life behind her and life churning through her veins—that is exciting!

I think the little starlets are adorable and pretty. Some of them could dress better. They don't have to show everything. But we all have gone through that and I cannot hold myself up as an example. I remember wearing see through tops back in the 80's—so it's learning, it's experience. You have to figure out what is appropriate for you. I prefer elegance myself. I like a good suit and I love beautiful colors and pretty blouses. You have to first look in the mirror and accept who you are. Acknowledge your fine points and don't worry about anything else. If you have great hair or great eyes, play those up. Visit the stores when they have the special cosmetic events and talk

"Be thankful, yes, but don't play Poor Pitiful Pearl. Be thankful for where you are, and tell people about your life."

to different people about their products. Find what looks best to bring out your inner beauty as well as your outer beauty. Highlight your best features and don't apologize for your others. For example, I have arthritis and I'm very self-conscious about my hands; one of my friends has made me very uncomfortable about my hands because they look old. They're all knobby and awful. Another friend of mine said, *"Well, I find your hands very expressive. Your hands have experience."* Well, when I'm on the stage, I gesture using my hands all the time, and she added, *"You don't see the knobs, because you use them with such eloquence. It is part of your life—it is an extension of who you are."* So now I look at this in a positive way.

Don't let yourself go. If you can possibly have your hair done, have it done. If you can, find a style that suits you, whether it's what the kids are wearing or not, experiment. Don't be ashamed of your glasses, have a lot of fun with them. I collect eye glasses. Find your own personal style. It's funny that the commercials use these twenty-five year olds to say, *"I use this cream to make myself look young."* Please, you're only twenty-five years old! You are young! Give me a break! It's hysterical. Why don't they just show a two year old and say, *"If you want baby soft skin..."*

When I was a teenager I used to say to my mom, *"How should I be at this party?"* Mother used to say, *"Just be your own sweet self."* Well, that didn't give me the answer I was looking for. What the hell is my own sweet self? I didn't know what to do and I was totally confused. *"Who am I? What is my own sweet self?"* I hadn't lived long enough to know, and I don't want to be a sweet self anyway.

I was so lucky to have wonderful, creative parents. They both had their audiences of course, daddy being a preacher, mother being a school teacher, and so I had to make my own audience. But they understood this desire, this creative thing in me, and I knew I was really lucky. No one could have been more supportive when I, their daughter, wanted to come to New York City and become an actress. When I first arrived in New York, daddy made sure to do his best and find me a safe place to live. He inquired through the Methodist church since he was a Methodist preacher. Through the church he found a home called the "Alma Matthews Home for Immigrant Girls," located on West 11th Street, and it was run by the "Women's Society of Christian Service." He got me a room there, and I paid $7.50 a week to board and have kitchen privileges.

The one thing I had to do in return was deliver talks and express my thanks to the various Women's Society of Christian Service chapters, located in different areas of New Jersey and Long Island. All the girls from the Alma Matthews Home would say, *"Oh it's so nice to be here, if it weren't for you I'd be on the streets,"* blah, blah, blah, and they just went on and on. When I would get up to speak, I'd just let my imagination run wild. I would say, *"Listen, you know what happened to me today? When I was going to the Neighborhood Playhouse, I got on the bus and asked for directions, but the driver didn't speak English."* I would just ramble on and say pretty much whatever came into my head. It was very entertaining and it was my way of keeping myself interested in what was going on. But the women at the Alma Matthews Home made me stop going because they said we laughed too much. And I said, *"Isn't that what we're supposed to do?"* Be thankful, yes, but don't play "Poor Pitiful Pearl." Be thankful for where you are and tell people about your life.

After 40 it became important for me to recreate myself. I started a new career in singing and writing. If I ever have time, I would love to take up a little painting and drawing. There's a store I often go past that sells all of these interesting artist materials; paints, brushes, pencils, oils and pastels. I love drawing, so that's something I definitely want to explore.

Happiness is achieved by expressing your full range of feelings, even sadness. You must do that. You can't cover it over because if you do, it will come out and bite you in the "you-know-where."

If I had to live life over again, I would do exactly what I've already done. I really have loved every moment of it—the good, the bad, and everything that has come with it. You don't have to settle, but I do believe in working and enjoying what you do. Live life to the fullest, and realize that this may be your last moment, so try and make it beautiful.

Put some money away. You don't have to buy everything you want. Don't be tempted to have what everyone else has. This is something that has been a real problem for me. Buy what looks best for you and buy only that one thing that's exceptional. If you buy too much, nothing will be special. You've got to appreciate what you've worked for and what you've got.

I've been guilty of shopping at Ferragamo, many times in the past, and bought God knows how many pairs of shoes. I have a picture taken with my little dog, Geraldine Page, sitting in a red Ferragamo shoe box. It was a darling picture of her. She was a Bijon, and was sitting amongst 100 pair of shoes. Some of them I never even wore, and now I wear only flats, and I still look great. I have a problem with my back, and it's not worth walking around in high heels just to appear stylish. If you want to be sexy, be sexy, but go barefoot. Get a nice pedicure—that's sexy—and indulge sometimes, if you can, in a massage.

We have got to do away with this peer pressure. Just because your best friend says something, that doesn't mean it's right for you. Don't hang around with people who put you down or make fun of you. Don't take it for a minute. Always consider the source. Negative comments and criticism often may be coming out of jealousy, because you are prettier, or taller, or have something the other person desires. Don't tolerate a single minute of it.

WHAT GOLDEN NUGGETS DID YOU GET FROM THIS TREASURE CHEST OF WISDOM?

_____

_____

_____

_____

_____

_____

_____

_____

ELLINE SURIANELLO

Leading Spokesperson on Women and Hair Loss
Founder of LeMetric Hair Center, Inc.
Age 53

How a woman changes physically as she ages is a big deal. Some women are much more accepting of those age related changes than others, and some women deal with it better than others. Since I've been in my line of work, dealing with women and hair loss, my facility has turned into this major therapy session and the hair becomes only one part of it. I thought, what a great platform, to talk about this with *Forty Plus and Fabulous* because that's the demographic of the majority of my clients. And so here they are, they're dealing with their hair, they're dealing with their body and especially now, with the economic changes. A lot of women haven't had to interview for a job in more than twenty years. A lot of women are going to be losing different parts of their lives, on top of the fact that their bodies are changing, on top of dealing with hormones, on top of the financial issues, on top, on, top, on top. So, I thought this would be a great opportunity to condense all the stuff I've done for the last twenty years, into this book.

Just how well a woman is able to cope positively with the physical changes will depend on where her self-esteem is. I'm 53 years old. We were in Philadelphia yesterday working, and my husband was there, along with some of the girls that work for me. We finished dinner and were leaving the restaurant. I'm probably 25 lbs. heavier than I was in my twenties, but my face is pretty much the same, and I take very good care of myself. As I'm walking out of the restaurant, this guy starts flirting with me. I started laughing and thought, *"Holy cow!"*

At my age, I think I look pretty good. I wasn't wearing a low cut top or anything short or revealing; I was just being who I am. It's about how I feel about how I look that comes across. I respect this body that God has given me. Isn't it interesting that even at this age, someone found me interesting enough or attractive enough to make a comment about me? It's not over until it's over, and that's exactly why I do what I do.

I have a 97 year old client who comes in with a walker, accompanied by her nurse and daughter. For her, going out to get her hair done is a big deal. She once said to me, *"Until I can't physically do it anymore, how I look is still important to me."* Physical appearance, for most women, is a very important element. If their self-esteem is still there, they want to be recognized. It's about the whole package; how you feel, how you look, how you smell, your voice—everything that makes you who you are. Maybe before, I would have said, *"Oh, how shallow it is to only think about how you look physically, or of only how you present yourself."* But I understand it really is the whole package. You are the whole package.

If a woman does not have a relationship with her spirit or soul, even more so than God or Spirit, she can't even realize the unconditional manner in which the Universe takes care of her. Nothing should be done in excess; I'm a big believer of that. So if you're drinking too much, or if you're smoking too much, it doesn't matter if you have a deep belief in God, you're ruining this temple.

Don't you believe you deserve to be healthy and have people notice you? What makes us not want to take care of ourselves? It's not just enough to believe that there's something greater than us. You have to do something with that belief. It is all about choices. Even with economic times being what they are now, we still have some choices. Look at the women who came over from Europe at the turn of the century, back in the 1800's. They still got dressed, they still had lives, and everything was much more difficult than it is now. So why are we falling apart? Did we forget who we are as women? I guess we got caught up in all this other stuff—the rings on our fingers, the cars we drive, the houses we live in. But right now, this excess is being taken away from all of us and we're being forced to re-examine ourselves.

This is the most wonderful era of my life because I get it now. I know why I'm here. It's not just about one part of me; it's about all these parts working together. Age doesn't have anything to do with it. It's your attitude towards life. The difference between where we are now, and where we were in our twenties is now we have life experiences to validate who we are. There are certain jobs and certain situations that you're not even qualified to be in when you're twenty because you simply don't have enough life experience.

By the same token, if you are 45, 50, 60, 70, or 80 years old and have not been willing to take a risk, or deal with your own fears, how do you attract people into your life, who are willing to take risks and deal with *their* fears? You don't, because

"JUST BECAUSE SOMETHING HURTS YOU DOWN TO YOUR SOUL, DOESN'T MEAN IT IS A BAD THING."

your growth is stunted and you continue to stay stuck. Take my 97 year old client for example; she doesn't need to come in and get her hair done, she could just wear a wig. But it's not about the hair; it's about the socialization aspect and her curiosity about what's going on around her. When you still have that, it doesn't matter how old you become.

The older you get and the more stuck you are—is when it begins to wear on you mentally, physically, psychologically and socially. That's where health issues come into play. It's also where loneliness becomes a factor, because no one wants to be around someone who is stuck, complaining, not moving forward, and has a gloomy outlook on life. Most people out there are not risk takers, but for those who are, it can also be very lonely.

The average person wants to play it safe, wants a steady 9-5 job, and wants to know that every Friday, they're going to get a paycheck. They need the security of knowing that their husbands are going to love them for the next 50 years. This can create really tough times for those who choose an illusion of safety, because there are no guarantees in life.

Getting to forty is a very important journey, and you should honor what you have gone through to get there, not discount it. Two top priorities should be to respect your health and not take your body for granted. Your body talks to you, whether you want to listen or not. My goal is to have an opportunity to say to women, *"Take care of yourselves."* Alcoholism among women is on the increase. We're drinking almost as much as men now, and that's scary.

Alcoholism and drug addiction is so rampant now because it provides a fantasy escape from reality. Prozac and Paxil are causing us not to feel anything anymore. Where is it said that we are not supposed to feel emotions? Have we become so soft that we don't want to feel anything?

I listen to my body. I move because movement, to me, is important. And I honor what I put in my body. I'm not big on junk food and never have been. You're a machine, and whatever you feed your body has to make it work. If it's a lot of junk, you're not going to feel good. But let's deal with reality here too. No one is going to spend several hours a day working out. Respect your body. If you're doing things in excess, try to figure out why.

It's time to know what makes you happy, what you want in life and what makes you feel good. For me, I feel most beautiful when I've done the best I know how to do. I feel most confident when people acknowledge that. I feel most alive when I'm laughing, and I feel my sexiest when someone a lot younger than me, flirts with me.

My hope is that women who have made it their mission to empower other women will band together, and let that journey continue, until we find other young women to take over. That's the beauty of life. You do what you need to do, while at the same time, empower other people to do what they're supposed to be doing, and then no one has to do anything by themselves. As difficult as certain things have been for all of us, it's usually during the most painful times in our life that we have learned the most valuable lessons. Embrace it. Just because something hurts you down to your soul, doesn't mean it is a bad thing. It means that there are all sorts of wonderful things that are going to happen because of these experiences. Embrace it.

WHAT GOLDEN NUGGETS DID YOU GET FROM THIS TREASURE CHEST OF WISDOM?

_____

_____

_____

_____

_____

_____

_____

_____

_____

NORMA HOLLIS

America's Leading Authentic Voice Doctor®

Age 63

B eing over 40 means that I'm not driven by hormones anymore. When you're younger, the hormones play such a dramatic role in your decision making and your day to day life and it can be very distracting. It can be enjoyable too but just trying to fulfill the demands of hormones is very distracting.

There also seems to be a little less confusion now about what it's all about. As I've grown older, I've become more settled and understand my purpose in life. I'm very Spirit driven and have been following the voices and energy that comes from within me, rather than the external ones.

For me, a woman is beautiful by whom she is on the inside; and by how connected she is with, not only her inner voice, but her ability to listen and follow the Spirit that lives within. I believe we're all born with gifts and talents, and a Spirit that directs us in how we use these gifts and talents. The beautiful women to me are the ones who have come to an understanding; to terms, to agreements, and to commitments to listen and feel that voice from within, and once they do, they have a certain glow about them. It doesn't matter what she looks like physically because it's her glow that is attractive and appealing, and draws others to her.

I believe the perfect body is a healthy body; one that you're comfortable in, and one that you're taking good care of. In return, it rewards you by giving you the ability to do the things you need to do in life.

If I have any concerns at this stage of my life, it would be not being able to fulfill what I was sent here to do. I feel, in many ways, that I have accomplished my primary mission, which is to create the authenticity movement, and all the pieces that helps people in the discovery and development of their natural gifts and talents.

"A WOMAN SHOULD DO WHAT MAKES HER FEEL BEAUTIFUL, AND FOR ME, WEARING LIPSTICK MAKES ME FEEL BEAUTIFUL."

My work is 30 years in the making and I feel like I'm just getting started. It's very fulfilling, when you become clear on your purpose, and I find my life now, to be much more satisfying and rewarding.

Changing my eating habits has been a very important accomplishment in my over forty lifestyle. My mother had colon cancer and three other female family members had digestive cancers. After personally taking antibiotics for forty years, it created an internal ecology of Candida, causing me to lose a lot of my energy. I finally realized that something with my body was not quite right. Since then I have eliminated beef, along with most meats, and have chosen a diet that consists largely of raw foods and quality water. Now I have become very conscious of what I put in my body. I've been blessed with a really good muscular system, so I have not had the need to work out much from an aesthetic standpoint. I am starting to see a little cottage cheese in my thighs and I can't stand it. I'm also feeling a little soft, and I can't stand that either. I walk, but I go through phases. For a while I will walk every day, and then I may go three months and not walk at all. Somehow, I always come back to walking and now my goal is to add light weight-lifting and resistance exercises to my program. I have a masseuse in LA who has told me that my body is more like that of a 35 year old.

Aging is a natural part of life, so why try to avoid what is natural? After all, what's the alternative? If you're not aging, you're in the ground, so embrace growing older and all the positive aspects that come with it. If we focus less on the wrinkles, the effects of gravity and the forgetfulness, we will see that there are some wonderful things about aging that we should embrace. As you get older, one should become more authentic and the greatest opportunity for authenticity happens with age—once you realize you've been through all the fake and phony stuff, and you can decipher through what's real and what's not. It's then a matter of choosing to embrace those things that are real and truly a part of you.

A woman should do what makes her feel beautiful, and for me, wearing lipstick makes me feel beautiful. It brings my color out and compliments the short hairstyle that I love to wear. I can have my makeup and earrings on, but it's the signature orange lipstick that really brings out my color and makes me pop, and that's when I feel the most beautiful.

Being in front of an audience is what I love best. It's what makes me feel my most confident and what I need to do more of. I'm breaking the old habits of sitting behind a desk because that's not where I belong. I want to be out in front of an audience, empowering and inspiring individuals to find greater levels of peace, contentment, joy, happiness and satisfaction.

Age is a gift. What greater gift? God gifts you only so many years. Look at the friends who didn't make it this far. The stress with aging comes when there is too much focus on the physical beauty, instead of on the inner beauty and the gift of wisdom that comes with age. So if anyone is struggling, chances are they're struggling because they're either looking solely at the physical aspects of aging, or the fact that the older you get, the closer you are to your transition, which is also a gift.

Don't be fearful of transition. Transition simply means you've done your job here on this planet and now you get to rest.

WHAT GOLDEN NUGGETS DID YOU GET FROM THIS
TREASURE CHEST OF WISDOM?

_____

_____

_____

_____

_____

_____

_____

_____

_____

_____

TERRY KOHL

President, Incredible Things
Media Management Marketing
Age 60

Hands up! Being over 40 is all about my favorite "F" words: *Fun & Fabulous Friends*; *Future* clear and tantalizingly, *Free* of youthful *Folly*; *Firm* in my beliefs and resolves; *Fertile* imagination and *Fervent* in my life's calling; *Faithful* to my dreams, and *Fashion* savvy; *Fantastically* healthy and deliciously *Feminine*.

Trust me—there has never been a more rewarding time in my life than now. It seems as though all the previous years were meant to culminate to this point, and have served to launch me into having the experiences, abilities and skill sets to live out a *Ferociously Fear*-less life! Y-a-a-y, me!

When I look at myself I don't see 60. It's really what you see on the inside, and we all do, whether we're conscious of it or not. If you're vital, healthy, and living life on purpose, you don't see 60 years, or 45, 57, or even 102. You see the "Shero" that's inside of you. True beauty comes from within. It's a beauty you can count on all the time. You might not be able to count on your hair not turning gray, or not getting some wrinkles. But the true beauty for all of us is in our hearts and our souls, and what we emanate beyond the makeup.

My mother always claimed that I exited from the womb selling. I'm not even sure what she meant by that—but apparently, I have a very gregarious nature and love to network and be around people. On the other hand, I have had some challenges that have set me back and have caused me to think about what direction I want to go in, *"Do I want to crawl under the covers and pull the blankets over my head?"* And there have been times where I seriously thought about it, but that just isn't me. It's much more like me to say, *"You know what? I'm not going to let this get to me. I'm going to figure out a way to accept this challenge and look at it from the standpoint of, this is really a gift I've been given, and do I want to open it and find out what the surprise is inside, or, do I just want to throw it*

"If you are in the driver's seat, it's a much better place to be, rather than screeching around corners, watching the world go by, when you don't have any control over the steering wheel."

away?" I love surprises too much, so I always open it! It becomes a habit once you start facing your challenges or fears, whatever you want to call them. You know it's not that scary when you embrace them.

I have such a great group of friends. I think that I gravitate towards people who have the same type of outlook on life as I do. It's pretty hard to be an outgoing, fun kind of person and then have someone in your circle that just doesn't get it. It's too much effort to drag them along when a part of having fabulous friends, is being fabulous and fun together.

I'm a networker, even in my own social environment. Every summer, I have a party called *Ladies on the Lawn*, and I invite all the women friends that I have, even if I just met them the day before. We all bring food and dress up in long flowing garden style clothing. I will allow only one man to attend. He is a friend who plays the fiddle, violin and the mandolin. He fiddles all afternoon, walking around the yard and serenading us. It is so much fun that I can't even begin to tell you. We just eat, gab, and listen to our one little man guy play music.

You have to create your own world, or your world is going to create one for you. If you are in the driver's seat, it's a much better place to be, rather than screeching around corners and watching the world go by, when you don't have any control over the steering wheel.

Oh, didn't we take ourselves so seriously when we were young? We thought we were so important. We had so many things to do and we were A-type personalities, or at least I know I was. I wasted a lot of time running around in circles and chasing things that had no substance. As we grow wiser, we tend to look at things with a little bit more of a careful eye. *"Is it really necessary for me to go down that road?"* We tend to observe more than react. At least, that's just what I'm hoping over 40 does for people. And when we observe *more* than we react, it's a whole lot more fun.

As you look at the world now through a much broader lens, I think you reduce the foolishness. Don't get me wrong, it was fun to have follies, but as you grow older, you start becoming a little more serious about what you are here to do. Fun should replace folly in some sense, and as I said earlier, I believe we create our own world. Once you understand that, you will be able to incorporate all of these fantastic "F" words into your life and just play with them.

We don't play enough as adults and it is so important. If you ever watch a child playing, they are not constantly looking at their watch, wondering whether to get supper ready or whether to do something else. They are so into the moment and it's such a delicious place to be. We've all experienced it—whether we've been painting, walking, or been so immersed in something that we really love to do, that we look at the clock and can't believe how much time has passed, and wonder, *"Where did the time go?" That's* being in the flow of the moment, doing what it is that brings you joy.

When you're flowing in those joyous moments, time just totally disappears. When we are not, we're always looking at the clock, hoping time will pass by quickly. Passion is another thing that we've lost somewhere along the way.

There's something else about being in the moment that we don't realize often enough, and that is, we never know how our attitude, our smile, our very essence, is capable of affecting total strangers. A couple of years ago, I was in a store, and I was just whistling and walking down the aisle, shopping. When I left the store, I was carrying my shopping bag and heading towards my car when I noticed this man out of the corner of my eye, running towards me. It startled me until he said, *"I have been waiting for you to come out of that store. I just wanted to tell you that watching you walking down the aisle and whistling just made my day. I was having a horrible day, then when I heard you, it reminded me of how much I loved to whistle as a kid, and from now on, I'm going to whistle whenever I feel stressed out!"* Now that was a pretty amazing thing! Before we leave the house we fix our hair, put on our make-up, and then we leave the house wearing a big grumpy frown on our face. What's that all about?

I have chosen a path that is not exactly filled with monetary compensation and that's because I love to help people. Don't get me wrong, I make a nice living and it's exactly what I need. I don't need anymore, and if I ever do, I'm sure that the Universe will provide it. But I'm very secure in knowing what I want to do with the rest of my life and it's such a relief to know that. I think when we come to the conclusion that we're here to help each other, it eliminates all the pressure. When we start looking for all the ways we can help one another, we start feeling better about ourselves. Then other people start feeling better about themselves too, because it's *that* contagious. At that point, we are back to having fun again.

It has taken me a while to come to find what my life's work is. But when we finally discover what it is we are here to do, it is such a great feeling. You can't help but be fervent about it.

You keep getting a reaffirmed spirit that, *"Yes, this is what you are supposed to do."*

Being faithful to your dreams doesn't mean that your dreams can't change. I am convinced that really great ideas are just dreams, waiting to be born. When I look at them that way, I realize how responsible it is to birth them, so that they can spread their joy. It really causes me to look at my dreams in a more serious manner.

I have always wanted to live to be 100 and now, my new goal is to reach 110. I am doing my part to stay physically healthy. I walk six miles a day and have been for 30 years now. I do yoga, love to go bicycle riding in the summer and I hike. Just being outdoors with nature is one of the best feelings in the world. I eat healthy and have been a vegetarian for 42 years. When I don't feel well, the first thing I look at is my internal barometer... my fun gauge. As a society, we use way too many drugs. We think that there is a quick fix for everything. Really, our quick fix is just looking inside sometimes and checking out what's going on internally, as opposed to wanting a pill to make us feel better.

I love being feminine. My girly-girl closet has things hanging all over the wall, and contains a colorful display of hats, scarves and necklaces. I am a firm believer in accessorizing, even if it is just a funky hat or a fun flowing scarf. I just love being a girl.

Life goes on until we die. There is no age that we reach where we cannot give all that there is to give.

There is no physical challenge that can keep us from giving if that's how we look at what makes up our life. In other words, if we look outside ourselves, get out of the victim mindset and look to see how we can help others, the years don't matter. That's because we aren't just about our age.

We're the accumulation of life and we get so many opportunities later on to use our wisdom to help others. That is something to look forward to, rather than regret that we are aging.

WHAT GOLDEN NUGGETS DID YOU GET FROM THIS TREASURE CHEST OF WISDOM?

_____

_____

_____

_____

_____

_____

_____

_____

_____

_____

_____

DR. JOHNETTA COLE

Director, National Museum of African Art, Smithsonian Institution
Age 73

I am not sure if in my much, much, much, much younger years I would have dared to walk into what I have just agreed to do. To go on an adventure which really requires not only faith—but, I think the Yiddish word would capture it best, *chutzpah!*

Here I am, the new Director of the Smithsonian's National Museum of African Art. I am not an Artist; I am African American, not African, and I am not a Curator. Yet, here I am doing something which fundamentally is in response to my passion for African Art, my respect for the people who made, and who today as contemporary artists make this work, and my conviction that art has enormous power to not just move and inspire, but to teach and be an instrument of change. We tend to associate risk taking with youth, but I find myself way beyond forty being a risk taker. Anything that is truly important in one's life you ought to have enormous respect for, and a little tinge of fear probably does not hurt. I certainly found myself saying over the years to my students at Spelman and Bennett College for Women, *"If you're nervous, if you're a little tense, if you're even a little afraid about taking on this college journey, that's a good thing. One should not take it lightly. One should not assume that it's a piece of cake."*

I am 73 years old. I certainly cannot address for other women what age is too "old" to reinvent themselves or start a new career. There is a danger in making a blanket statement that all women "should". However, if a woman does not raise that question for herself, it is a very serious mistake.

Because I have done what I have done, and that is to walk into a new arena of work at age 73, that doesn't mean that I think every woman should do this. I do think that every woman ought to think, *"Should I? Do I want to? Can I, with a degree of satisfaction?"*

I remember growing up in Jacksonville, Florida with a lot of input from the community that grew me. One of the things I was always told, *"Beauty is as beauty does"* and I truly believe that.

Even for individuals who are endowed with what is stereotypically called "beauty," if that individual does not move through the world thinking of others, being of service to others, then all of that external, physical attractiveness, is shamefully wasted in my view, because beauty is as beauty does. And, while I don't think we should avoid talking about people who are attractive, beautiful, lovely or handsome, I am far more interested in what people do, than how they look. We don't want to act as if personal adornment is irrelevant. I'm now the Director of an art museum which certainly in some way, but not exclusively, is about differing definitions of beauty, differing definitions of power and differing definitions of relationships. So I don't want to sound as if I think personal adornments are irrelevant or sinful.

"AND SO, RATHER THAN SPENDING THAT AMOUNT OF TIME TRYING TO REINVENT ONE'S SELF PHYSICALLY, THINK WHAT COULD BE DONE IF ONE WERE REINVENTING ONESELF INTERNALLY."

DR. JOHNETTA COLE

I really enjoy each morning, or sometimes given my schedule I have to do this at night, thinking about what I will wear, not only because I need it for warmth or I need it to be as cool as possible in a heat filled day, but I think about the color and the texture that I will enjoy seeing on myself, and that I wish others will enjoy. I like to do makeup, but I am not going to spend the biggest hunk of my time invested in all of that. Those same folk who grew me in Jacksonville had a lot of ways of saying, *"Everything in moderation, don't go overboard,"* or a million other ways of saying if you've got to inject stuff in your lips, or as a Jewish woman, decide you have to have a nose job, or the Asian woman, who has to change the contour and the slant of your eyes for somebody else's notion of your beauty, in my view, that's just sad. The days in which black women, and it was not just a few of us, used skin lightening cream, is a statement that is very, very sad to me. And so, rather than spending that amount of time trying to reinvent one's self physically, think what could be done if one were reinventing oneself internally.

One of the most important things I've done for myself after forty is discover the joy of exercise. I remember once, when being interviewed, the person asked me what I regretted not having done in my youth. My answer was I didn't much before forty really discover the joy in exercise. I still, some mornings, get up and say, *"I don't want to do that."* But once I do, there's something there; a very, very good feeling. Exercise is one of the top three things I do for my health. I also try to eat in a sensibly good way. I would tell a tale if I say I try to get enough sleep, because I still don't get enough sleep but, I do spend some time each day in a combination of meditation and prayer. I believe our physical selves are connected with other parts of who we are.

When I was about to go off in my twenties to do field work, which was necessary for me to get a PhD in Anthropology, I was going to Liberia and West Africa. I was petrified. I had then, but much less now, a phobia about chickens. I went to a fellow graduate student who was also a trained Psychiatrist, and said to him, *"Put me on the couch, I am so afraid of going to Liberia, because there are going to be chickens everywhere."* And, he replied, *"No, I won't do it. Actually, amongst us graduate students, you're probably the most centered. But this, I will tell you. I will tell you what fear is, and then, I want you to realize that this will be of some help to you." He said, "Fear is the inability to put yourself into a situation to see that there is nothing to fear."* And he was right.

Over time, when I had no choice, I was in situations with those awful chickens and I came to see, not completely, but that there was less to be afraid of. As it relates to aging, you're going to go there anyway... if you're lucky. And so, moving through these decades of life, you will learn, I hope, as I learned, that there's nothing there to fear.

The worst part is the prelude; the worst part is before you get there. But once there, I hope you are able to see, that aging is not only an inevitable process, but it can be a very moving, rewarding, and in many ways, exciting process.

WHAT GOLDEN NUGGETS DID YOU GET FROM THIS TREASURE CHEST OF WISDOM?

_____

_____

_____

_____

_____

_____

_____

KIM CAMERON

Singer/Songwriter Side FX Band

Age 42

I have just recently figured out that I'm actually over forty. It's really a matter of how you feel about yourself. Perhaps if I felt I couldn't physically do the same things I could do twenty years ago, then I might feel like I have aged. I feel smarter now, and feel fuller and happier as a person. I have embraced this time of my life. I don't know if it has to do with being over forty, but I'm just a happier person now.

I actually don't want to leave my forties although, I wouldn't want to go backwards either. I don't know what's coming at fifty plus—maybe it will be even better. But I like this time of my life. In my mind, you still look like you did in your thirties, and I don't think women really look as good as they do until they get past their thirties.

When you're in your forties, you tend to look more distinguished. Look at any of your magazines or even recent pictures of your friends; they're so much more attractive looking now than they were when they were younger. I wouldn't trade the time from a purely aesthetic point of view, or even from an intellectual point of view. I'm just a lot smarter now, thank goodness, and I think I react better to people.

When I recall some of my reactions to people, especially to family or friends or coworkers, it was very extreme. It was either super-happy, or super-sad, or super-upset, and it really didn't place things into perspective. Now, I'm more relaxed about a lot of things. It allows me to be a little bit more open as far as listening to people and being genuinely interested in what they have to say.

The older a woman becomes, the more precise she is about how she feels about something. She is able to relate better, and just in my small world of music, she is able to connect lyrics to things that are going on in her life, regardless of what that story might ultimately be about, she can take that and use it as an outlet. We think about things on a much deeper level than men do. We are more in line with being deep thinkers, and the more experienced and the more confident we become as we grow older, we think about things a little more deeply and we apply these thoughts to our lives.

"I HAVE MUCH MORE MEANINGFUL CONVERSATIONS WITH MY GIRLFRIENDS NOW, PARTLY BECAUSE WHEN I WAS YOUNGER I DIDN'T KNOW HOW TO DESCRIBE HOW I FELT, AND PARTY BECAUSE I WAS AFRAID TO DESCRIBE HOW I FELT."

The most interesting facet about women is that they are able to be themselves and acknowledge all of their accomplishments. Listening to their stories is one of my favorite things to do. It's why women like to get together, because they like to share their stories and feelings with one another.

Women need to have an outlet with other women. As you get older, your friendships become more and more important, and people are better at nurturing them, because you have more time to do that. When you're running around in your twenties and thirties and you're still trying to figure out who you are and what you want to do with your life, and you're trying to keep up with family obligations and kids, your friendships can slip away. I have found deeper relationships in my existing friendships that I've formed from thirty-nine on, than prior to that time. That was because back then, I was trying so hard to climb the corporate ladder, get married and all of those things, and I probably short circuited and lost a lot of valuable time with my friends. I have much more meaningful conversations with my girlfriends now, partly because when I was younger I didn't know how to describe how I felt, and partly because I was afraid to describe how I felt.

I made a very bold move after my forties, and couldn't have done it beforehand. I wish I had the nerve to do it when I was younger, but there was no way I was capable of doing so, because I lacked the confidence I needed. The catalyst, a young family members fight for his life, made me re-evaluate my life's work.

That, I think has less to do with age and more to do with the fact that women need time to feel like they're worth something, and I definitely took all that time to decide that I was worth something. We spend so much time trying to find out who we are in our twenties and then trying to prove ourselves in our thirties.

By the time we reach our forties, we have gone through both of those cycles. Now we can affirm, *"I know who I am, I know what I want to do and I can accomplish and do anything I desire, if I set my mind to it."* I could not have done that in my twenties, and I certainly could not have done it in my thirties. I firmly believe it's all about having the will to succeed, and striving until you finally reach that dream. Pursue what you really want to do without placing a time limit on how long it will take you to get there. Pursue what you truly believe in and then the pursuit itself will feel very gratifying.

When I embarked on my music career, hoping to become a songwriter and have my own label, I had lots of exposure on multiple fronts. It was a challenging time for me, and sometimes very painful. While I would have loved to have been able to say, *"Okay, I'm now 100% profitable after only 6-7 months doing this full time,"* that's just not the reality. If I had set a goal that it absolutely had to be done within the first six or seven months, I would have deemed myself as a failure.

One reason I was able to get established in my music career is my time commitment. I am probably putting in eighty hours per week on making this work because I enjoy it so much and I'm so determined that I don't even realize I'm putting that much time into it.

I have found that chasing a dream is so intense and so powerful. It overtakes you and gives you an inner strength you otherwise wouldn't have. If I had done this when I was thirty, would I have had this driving ambition? I don't think so. I think I would have pulled out saying, *"Okay, I should have had much more significant results in my pursuit these past six months, and I didn't, so I better drop back."* I didn't have the confidence back then to say, *"You know, I'm going to keep striving, because it feels right, and I believe in myself."* I think we are a little smarter when we reach forty because we can now say, *"You know what? You've got to give it time, be a little patient, let yourself figure out how to do this, and adjust and accept these challenges."*

Figure out some marketing strategies and bring some people on board who are smarter than you are and you're going to become smarter as you go through the learning process along with them. I'm 98% sure that in my thirties my reaction would have been, *"I just can't do it. I don't know why I pursued it. It was stupid and I can't continue."*

With the collapse of many companies, and the huge number of people losing their jobs, it is certainly a tough time. Do not be fearful of being over forty if you're out there looking for a job. I hired someone in my small business to assist in the process. She is a great, young go-getter type of gal. Having previously worked in the corporate world with people my age, there is something inherent that happens when approaching forty. I have a tendency to be a little biased towards women because I feel that women work harder, especially women over forty. They just catch on faster.

Having been the boss of many individuals in my life, both male and female, I can say to a forty year old, *"Here is the information, and this is what I need you to do,"* and that's about all the conversation that's needed. I can give the same information to a twenty-five or twenty-six year old, using the same amount of energy, and it will take three or four conversations with them to complete the same task. You're just so much smarter after forty, and in the corporate world, that's a huge value to an employer. It's certainly a huge value to me, having worked formerly as a manager, and now as the owner of a music label. When you walk in the door, you know that things are being handled properly, and that's a significant plus.

I remember a great line from a movie, *"Marriage makes women messy,"* and I think that is so true, it does make women messy. The first marriage was just stupid. I felt like I should have gotten married just because I was young, had fallen in love and thought that it was appropriate at the time. Given the choice to do it over, I certainly would not have made that same choice. I married again, thinking that this time, I'm going to do it for all the right reasons, and I think I have. If something were to happen, would I crumble at being single again? I don't think so. I think that has a lot to do with being forty, and having confidence, and knowing that whatever happens, life goes on. Is it great to have a spouse around to be able to share things with? Without a doubt! Even though men are different from women, they still provide some very particular comforts.

I find that I am definitely less needy now, and I think that's because I am more comfortable with myself. I've become more capable to be able to reach out to people when I need support. I don't want to give the impression that there is anything wrong with being needy, but it does come down to the basic fundamentals of having confidence. I did have that neediness earlier in life, but in my late thirties, it dawned on me that it was not there anymore.

The physical changes that occur with aging aren't fair, but most of life is not fair—so, I think it's appropriate that we have to deal with it. Don't let yourself go. Exercising and eating right makes a huge difference in your physical appearance, and those are things that everyone can do. Gravity is eventually going to take over, but keeping yourself up is a big part of our responsibility as women and as human beings.

I think women start looking better with a little gravity under their skin. The beauty I have seen in my friends is just remarkable from what it was fifteen years ago. They're just more interesting to look at. Do they have a few wrinkles? Yeah, they have a few wrinkles. But the wrinkles aren't something that bothers me. I can tell you, that when we go out for a girls weekend in New York or Las Vegas, none of us have any trouble attracting attention. It all has to do with attitude. If you are confident about yourself and the way you look, it shows. You express it through your attitude, in your face and your body. I think men are more interested in interesting women.

There's a total difference between looking old and acting old—and none of my friends act old, and I think that's the key. It's almost like a magnet, and you can't help but be attracted to it. I love being on stage, and have recently taken note of the reactions I get from younger men. I once played at a college bar, and these guys were swarming up to me, and I remember thinking, *"This is unbelievable!"* They were no more than twenty-two, or twenty-three years old, and they were asking me for my phone number, and it was really very flattering. It has happened to me many more times in the last couple of years. I don't ever remember getting that reaction in my thirties, or even in my twenties, I only had older guys who would talk to me. There were rarely any guys my age, so go figure.

Cher said she experienced the same thing. One of my backup singers just performed with me as a one-time favor. She is 49 years old, and after the performance, four guys, of all different ages, came up to me and asked me if they could ask her out. So, believe me, it ain't over 'til it's over.

WHAT GOLDEN NUGGETS DID YOU GET FROM THIS
TREASURE CHEST OF WISDOM?

_____

_____

_____

_____

_____

_____

_____

_____

_____

_____

TANYA HUTCHINSON

Model, Reality TV Winner, *She's Got the Look*

Age 47

I think I'm 100 percent wiser now, and there's no shame in my game. I'm at a stage where I feel really good about where I've been, where I am presently, and confident about what lies ahead. I have no regrets about leaving my twenties and thirties behind, and there's nothing from my youth that I would want to go back and recapture.

In my youth, I would never have had the confidence to participate in a show like *"She's Got the Look."* I say that because as a teenager, I was brutally attacked by a gang of girls who used razors to slash my face, neck, chest and arms. The wounds required 100 stitches, and were not only damaging to me physically, but affected my confidence and self esteem as well. It was a very trying time as a thirteen year old.

After the attack, I became very withdrawn. I grew my hair long to cover the scar on my check, and wore turtlenecks to cover the rest. I was always ashamed to talk about the past, to talk about the things that happened, and to show my scars. It was in college that I was finally able to begin to go through the healing process of overcoming it and began to slowly find my inner beauty and strength.

I feel that there's beauty in having grey hair and wrinkles; I long to have mentorships from women who feel good about aging. It's important that we have mother and grandmother figures to look up to who are filled with wisdom and knowledge from their life experiences. I have a mother-in-law who is just fabulous, and she looks great for her age and is a super confident woman. That to me is what makes a woman beautiful. It's having confidence in her abilities, accepting her weaknesses and flaws. It's creating a balance between her inner and outer beauty. I'm not intimidated by women who are more beautiful or smarter than I am or who make more money than I do. In fact, I want those women to be my friends so I can learn the tricks of the trade and improve. I love surrounding myself with women who are movers and shakers and are going places.

"FORGIVENESS IS MANDATORY, AND VERY LIBERATING. WHEN YOU FORGIVE SOMEONE ELSE, THEY NO LONGER HAVE POWER OVER YOU."

You're never too old to become what you might have been. I've been in the modeling and beauty industry for years, and I think society has changed, and that age is an old school way of thinking.

I am at a place where I can say, *"Okay, now I can retire from modeling, because I feel that I've achieved the pinnacle of success, and now, I want to get out of the modeling industry."* I'm going to go out on a positive note. My contract is up this year, and then I plan to officially retire. Right now though, I need to continue working, and don't have the luxury of retiring. My husband has been laid off twice in the past three years, and he's been out of work for the past eight months. You could say, *"Okay, he's been the income earner, I've been at home with the kids and I don't have anything to offer."* But nothing could be farther from the truth!

Now's the time to dig deep inside and find out what really fuels you. We're not what we used to be, the forties are the new thirties, and because of technology, science, anti-aging products and the fact that we're more aware of health issues, we still can feel and look young as we continue to grow older, as long as we still have something to offer in life.

I recently asked myself, *"What can I do, where I can earn a decent salary, be challenged, both mentally and physically and where do I go from here?"* So, at the age of forty-seven this year, I've decided that I'm going to become a Deputy Sheriff. I am in the pre-academy training program now, and in the hiring stage. It's been a grueling process, but I welcomed the challenge. They didn't set an age limit. They explained to me that as long I passed the time test, can do the push-ups, sit-ups and meet the other requirements, that I would qualify. I am so confident that I am going to become a Deputy Sheriff in about 6-7 months! Initially, I had concerns thinking, *"What are the age requirements? Can I still do this at my age and keep up with those twenty year olds?"* I'm now competing against men and women who have served in the military, some just recently graduated from high school and some are in college. It's exciting that I have maintained my health and can still hang with the best of the best.

I have a daughter and four sons, and my boys especially, are so excited about my new career. They can't wait to hear my stories when I come home, after working in the prison all day or walking my beat on the street. My kids are so interested in my job, and I'm fueled by their enthusiasm, and at the same time, proud that I am able to contribute and support my family.

Forgiveness is mandatory and very liberating. When you forgive someone else, they no longer have power over you. Harboring resentment can make you feel weak, or even ill, and can cause other problems. When you learn to forgive others and not hold a grudge, that's a sign of maturity. It's very beautiful to be able to forgive. These are a couple of the most important things that I've done for myself after turning forty. That's when you still love the people who have caused you problems, or even forgive your mother and not blame her anymore for things that went wrong in your life. That's when you take ownership and responsibility and accountability; when you make a mistake, you can say, *"Yeah, it's my mistake...and?"* You own up to it and you move forward. So accept your shortcomings and don't blame others. Don't allow your age or other people to be your crutch in life.

Come to grips with reality, since we are supposed to age. That's the life cycle, and the one that God created for us. It's a little shocking initially, when you start noticing the first few lines and wrinkles on your face. I'm going to the gym regularly, and after doing all these crunches, I wonder why my skin is still flabby? It's an adjustment to see yourself now in a different light. Once you accept that this is where you are, then do the best that you can with what you have been given. I'm not the best eater, and I still like baked goods and sweets, but I also know what changes I need to make in my diet. When I have to be in front of the camera, you better believe I'm stepping up my game, watching what I eat and doing some extra cardio.

When comparing yourself to other women, be aware of your motives. Most of the time, what you see in magazines is just an altered image. It has been touched and retouched and it's not a true, realistic representation of what someone actually looks like. There are a lot of people who are just naturally gifted with great genes. They can eat whatever they want, do whatever they want, and still look great. Don't compare yourself to others. Set standards and realistic expectations for yourself. It's inspiring to see the over forty images of models and actresses still showcased in magazines today.

Life is a constant learning, shedding and growing experience. You never arrive, and you're never finished, and that's the whole point. If you slow down, it's only for a moment. Continue to sharpen your craft and learn new trades.

I don't have all the answers and I don't know what tomorrow brings, but I know that whatever it is, I can face it because I have God on my side. I'm at a place in my life now where I can take a bullet for somebody, and I'm not afraid to die.

TANYA HUTCHINSON

What golden nuggets did you get from this treasure chest of wisdom?

_____

_____

_____

_____

_____

_____

_____

_____

_____

_____

_____

_____

_____

ROSELLE WILSON

Owner, Lady Marian's Wearable Art
Age 60

I feel a freedom that I've always dreamed of—a freedom to be able to do the things I want to do; to choose the situations I am a part of; to be able to bring a certain wisdom to a situation; to be able to translate and transmit a sense of the history that we have as women, and particularly, as African American women. To be able to bring these things with a sense of style and grace, that only comes with age.

I am first and foremost a unique individual. I haven't found another one like me, and I'm still waiting for that person to show up. But I am unique in the sense that I have done a lot of things that other people say they want to do, but don't have a plan for doing. I've traveled half way 'round the world. I still have the other half yet to go, and I'm not finished. I've immersed myself in cultures and styles that people manifest all over the world. And I enjoy people. As an adult female, I see myself as a trailblazer more than a role model. I'm a trailblazer for people to be able to follow, kind of leaving the signs or the guidepost, if you will, along the way that people don't have to struggle as much as they do.

In this day and age, struggling is just a draining force in life so, to the degree that people don't have to struggle, I want to show them how to make life less strenuous, so that they can fulfill their dreams with all the energy they can muster.

With the passage of time, I can say I know myself more. I have a better and broader outlook on life. I think the first half of your life, you're focused on you; what you want, what you need, what makes you happy, or what makes you angry. It's all about you.

I have found that it's so much more rewarding to already know that part, to be able to articulate it and move on. It's not about me; this is about the future generations and who we give life force to.

I know I am a part of that generation where, it was all about me, and I have broken away from that, to look at how it impacts and affects others. It is our responsibility to pass on our history, our style, our generosity as women, family and leaders, in all the roles that we take on. Women in particular, take on such a vast variety of roles that we almost forget who we are in the process. When we know who we are, we can focus on other people and bring our true selves to that situation.

"THE TWINS ARE EVENTUALLY GOING TO DROP AS GRAVITY TAKES OVER— SO JUST TAKE YOUR BRA OFF AND LAUGH AT IT."

Giving birth to my boutique, "Lady Marian's," came to me as a concept probably thirty years ago, as I broke out of the boring corporate mold of wearing three piece suits and high heels. I started to notice that there was very little beauty, style, or culture, associated with that look. At the time, I was immersed in my African and Native American culture, and I wanted to be able to proudly display that. I made incremental changes at first, and then it became my way of dressing. Sometimes people understood, and at other times, they would question or challenge what I was wearing. But that's who I am and that's what I bring, and if it's not what you're interested in then, I'm sorry. I grew beyond that, and people starting saying, *"I want to shop in your closet."* Well that was opening up a big Pandora's Box for me. I told them, *"One of these day's I'm going to open a store and you can come shop there."* That seed was planted in my brain over twenty-five years ago, when I was just about to turn forty.

I continued working until I turned 59 because, as a single parent, I needed to. I was the Vice President of two universities, during my fifties, which was not particularly traditional for women, especially African American women, and I was successful at both of these institutions.

When it came time to retire I thought, *"Well, now is the time to open my store."*

The "Lady Marian's Boutique" is named after my mother, Marian, who has since gone on to the other side, but I constantly feel her spirit present in the store with me. She enjoyed seeing me in all the different patterns, colors, various outfits and cultural pieces, and was always excited about everything I had. Her inspiration helped me in creating every detail of the shop, and I wanted to honor her by placing the boutique in her name.

There is never an age when one cuts off life, and you should continue growing and recreating yourself. Life is a journey, and you have the power to do things that make a difference in your life and influence others. Lady Marian was a prime example of someone who didn't stop living until the day she died.

Six months before she died at age 95, she was on a three week cruise up the west coast of Africa, and she got off at Lisbon, Portugal.

She constantly traveled, and this is why I have the wander lust in me. Even when she was working, we would spend summers traveling all over the United States, Mexico and Hawaii. I had covered all but three states in the United States, when I began traveling overseas; starting with Africa, then Europe, South America, the Islands and Alaska. I have not made it to the Asian countries yet, but that's on my list of thing's to do. My mother traveled up until six months before she died, even though she was handicapped. She had to use a wheelchair and a walker to get around and needed an aide to accompany her. She was a strong woman, and lived her life to its fullest until the very end.

It was not until after my forties that I came to appreciate the art, the culture and the society of my ancestors. I began to read, travel, study and immerse myself in different cultures. I've built a library in my home filled with all kinds of history and culture, containing books, readings, tapes and videos. I've made it my business to learn all about my culture because it's not something we teach in our educational system, and it's certainly something our children could benefit from. I have made it my business to read and know as much as I can about my history and culture so that I can share this information with others.

I haven't accomplished all that I have set out to do, but I define success differently now than when I was younger. It's not about how much you accumulate or what the level of abundance might be in your life. That comes with time and good judgment, but it's not the center point.

Success has been redefined in that sense for me. I can become satisfied, fulfilled and happy, very quickly, and without a lot of thought or energy put into it. I am simplifying life as I know it every day, and the simpler the better. I'm not dealing with a lot of the madness around me in the environment, and I find myself more content and more at peace. I'm satisfied without relying on someone else to make me happy. I can manage my own happiness, because I know who I am. That's not being arrogant; it's just that I don't require a lot to make me happy. I like people and being around them, but emotionally, I'm fine by myself as well.

I was born an only child, and most of my formative years were spent in solitude, but not in a negative way. I had to teach myself how to be alone and be content with aloneness; not loneliness, but aloneness. I know that I can always reach out to other people, and people gravitate to me as well. On the flipside, I need to know when to pull off of that highway periodically and recharge my battery. My energy comes from within, and when I give of myself to others, I sometimes become emotionally drained, and then have to take the time out to rejuvenate myself, so that I can continue to give once again.

You don't know yourself until you're in your forties. You begin to comprehend who you are and where you fit in the world's scheme of things. You start to realize and identify where you have control, or don't have control over your circumstances or situations. You start making different types of decisions at forty and begin looking at life, people, and things in a different way. Preferably, in a more mature way, since everyone doesn't develop at the same rate. There are fifty year olds who still haven't "found themselves," yet, and that's because they either haven't tried hard enough, or perhaps no one has given them the tools in order to accomplish this.

There is a process in self-development, where you're either going in one direction or the other. It's not about standing still, because the dynamics of life prevent that from happening. You're either going forward in life with some tools that make sense, or else you're falling behind.

There is no reason why you can't do something to improve yourself. Don't compare yourself to others, because everyone is different, and it's such a counterproductive thing to do. There's no reason why you can't take care of you. Eating healthy is a good start, and exercising is even better. You've got to take these things on as though your life depends on it, because it certainly does. There are some things you can't prevent however, and those are things that will inevitably happen. The twins are eventually going to drop as gravity takes over—so just take your bra off and laugh at it. You can have as much surgery as you want or invest in all the expensive maintenance pieces you desire. Exactly what and how much, is your choice.

I visit spas, but I'm not trying to recreate what God gave me. This is the body I was born with, and this is the body I'm going out with. I'm not trying to recreate God's package, but I do want to make sure I take care of it because it's the only one I have. I'm grateful for this body, because I know it could have been a whole lot worse. I mean, what are you going to do, fret about it all day? No! I've got more important things to think about and accomplish in life. I can be content with myself, knowing I've done all the preventive maintenance I can possibly do to stay in shape, but eventually I realize that age will catch up with me, and I have to learn to accept the physical changes that come along with that. I can't spend a whole lot of time dwelling on it, and I refuse to, because there are some things we just have no control over.

You can stay in the gym as long as you want and still, some things just ain't gonna be right at the end of the day! I've seen people end up in a cycle of surgeries and it's never enough, they just end up wanting more. There are so many procedures available now; from Liposuction, tummy tucks, to Botox treatments. Sometimes it becomes an addiction and people are never content, and continue to have even more liposuction, tummy tucks, butt tucks, breast implants and even facial reconstructions.

A little color to cover the grey doesn't hurt, but since I'm not going to restructure anything, the only thing I can do at this point is laugh. So ladies, accept the inevitable; grey hair, wrinkles, memory loss, low libido, weight gain, hot flashes, and just learn to laugh and enjoy it!

WHAT GOLDEN NUGGETS DID YOU GET FROM THIS TREASURE CHEST OF WISDOM?

KIM HARRIS

Training and Development Consultant
SBA Women in Business Champion Recipient
Age 50

I have attained a level of confidence over the years that makes being over forty the absolute best time of life for me. In my younger years, twenties through early thirties, I was too busy trying to prove a point to other people, and too busy trying to show myself to be acceptable. What was missing was that I didn't accept myself. At this stage of the game I have come to fully accept myself, along with all my flaws and idiosyncrasies, and simply embrace who I am, for what I am, and present that to the world. Those who accept it, great! Those who don't, oh well! I have a different level of confidence about who I am at this stage, and I love it, because it allows me to be authentic. It allows me to be genuine in every way and not dissuaded by external voices. I can stay true to me.

There was one period in my life that was very dark, emotionally dark. I did not feel that I deserved anything good in life. I did not feel like I was worthy of anything good, and that everything just always had to be bad; had to be a challenge; and always had to be a fight. I finally came to a place where I realized that I don't have to fight anymore. I can put down the boxing gloves and move through my circumstances or situations with grace and dignity, and still come out a winner.

I move forward, knowing that challenges are always going to be there and present themselves; not to set me back, but to help me grow, and to help me stretch, help me see another dimension of myself and to help me express myself in another way.

"I CHANGED MY MIND ABOUT HOW I SAW MYSELF. I CHANGED MY MIND ABOUT HOW I SAW MY LIFE. I CHANGED MY MIND ABOUT WHAT I BELIEVED ABOUT ME."

I believe that there is not enough transparency. There are a lot of women out there who have gone through some challenges and really made their lives significantly important, yet they haven't shared their stories with others. A lot of it is because they attach to their experiences such shame, embarrassment or a perception of judgment. I feel it's important to share just a little glimpse of some of the challenges I've gone through, because I am not perfect. I'm here to tell you that if I can move through it, you can move through it too. This book will open the eyes of a lot of women in terms of how they feel and perceive themselves, especially with all the external pressures brought on by our society and what "aging" truly means. In my opinion, age is just a number. I have never felt better, sexier, more vibrant, confident or more capable than I do right now!

At one point, things became very dire for me financially, and I was technically homeless for about six months or so. Look, I was living, literally, on $375 per month, and anybody in their right minds, in this day and age, knows that it is nearly impossible to survive on that, but that's what I was doing. Although I was going through a rough period in my life, I still had food on my table, a roof over my head, clothes on my back, and my son was getting to school every day. I had gas in my car, and my bills were being paid. I didn't miss a beat. And it wasn't because of anything I was doing. It was all because God allowed people to come into my life and pull me through it, so I wouldn't sink back into that dark place again. He wanted me to understand that through the power of prayer, faith, and determination—you can get through anything.

"Change your mind, change your life," and that's just what I did. I changed my mind about how I saw myself. I changed my mind about how I saw my life. I changed my mind about what I believed about me.

My view on relationships is significantly different today, than it was when I was younger. My view on friendships back then was more about competition. Nothing was real, and everything was superficial. Today, the friendships I have are truly based on my discrimination for authenticity. My friendship circle is small. We love each other, we respect one another, we support each other and those are the kinds of friendships I want.

Now the physiological changes are a challenge, I'm not going to lie. Thank God for surgery, and thank God for the Board of Cosmetology and Plastic Surgeons. Not that I've done anything, although some day I might consider it as my body changes. Society has a lot to do with our perception of our bodies. I am all for being in shape and taking care of myself, eating healthy and exercising. Recently, I've lost 17 pounds, and overall a total of 30 pounds since last year when I first started because my health was borderline. I was not doing well with my heart. Heart disease runs rampant in my family, so I really jumped on the band wagon to get myself in shape and get back to a healthy place. It's been a long journey, but I would rather do it slowly and gradually than try to do it fast and have nothing last. I've been exercising and doing different things to keep my body in shape, but despite that, the physiological changes are going to occur as a natural response to aging.

With women, it seems we tend to experience many of the physiological changes much earlier than men do. They say that when women age, we get old, but when men age, they become distinguished. How did that happen? I started graying when I was twenty-six, and that runs in my dad's side of the family, where the women start to gray in their twenties, and by the time they reach thirty-five and forty, they have a full head of silver-gray hair. So, that has been a challenge. But again, thank God for hair color, because I've been using it for a long time. I could probably go gray and be okay, but ump-umm, I'm not ready for that, so I deal with it.

The other thing is this; I don't have a big problem with sagging skin, but the one thing I seriously do have a problem with, are my breasts. The girls are taking a trip down south, and I am not digging that at all. This is not cool, because it doesn't match my personality, it doesn't match my lifestyle and it doesn't match the rest of my body, to be quite honest with you. I don't need implants, but I am seriously considering the breast lift thing. The doctor that I've talked to, has told me that there are women twenty years younger than me who have problems worse than I do, and I can't imagine that. He told me that I didn't need a lift, but I want one for my own confidence and my own personal reasons. I'm just not comfortable with how things are transpiring at the top part of my body, and that's just one of the challenges that I'm faced with. There are great bras out there that do wonderful things for you, but at some point, you come out of your clothes, and if that's going to be the case then, hmmm, I kind of want to look the same out of the bra, as I do in it.

My attitude about work and career has changed significantly as well. Years ago, I thought you had to climb the corporate ladder in order to be successful. Back then, I didn't know any better. I sought jobs I would excel in, and thought would give me prestige and position. I went in there and started playing the political games and hated it, and after that, they were just jobs to me. I reached a place in my life where I was tired of working for someone else, and really desired to create something just for myself. Today, even though I work, I choose to work contract employment—so I pretty much establish the schedule for when I work and what hours I work. Even though there are core hours, I won't be there before a certain time, and you can expect I'll be the first out of the door at 5:00.

What I've learned is, it's not about having an attitude of arrogance; it's really an attitude of knowing what you want and knowing how to get others to give you what you want. You bring a tremendous value to their company, their team, or whatever it is you are contributing to—and because I know I can bring a certain level of usefulness to them, I can make demands and they'll accept them. I can get the money I ask for because I know my worth now. Back in the day, I was scared to death to ask for a ten cent raise; but today I go in with numbers. It's a very different attitude, but it's an attitude built on the level of confidence I have in my ability to bring value to them.

To the women who read this book and glean some of the experiences of the women who have been interviewed, I would say, *"Appreciate where you are, wherever that is. Because where you are, is where you need to be right now, in order to get to where you've got to go. It may not be what you like, it may not be close to where you thought you would be, but it's where you need to be; and, being where you need to be, is better than being where you want to be, especially if you're not ready to be there."*

WHAT GOLDEN NUGGETS DID YOU GET FROM THIS TREASURE CHEST OF WISDOM?

_____

_____

_____

_____

_____

_____

_____

_____

BRENDA POLLARD

Educator, Memphis City Schools
State and National Educational Presenter on Teaching At-Risk Youth
Age 47

B eing over forty is truly the best part of my life, because I feel like I am finally grown enough to do whatever I want to do, and better yet still, say what I want to say. If I need to say to someone, *"You're not going to speak to me that way,"* I say it now with some attitude and conviction behind it. You can't be fabulous when you're holding back.

One of the things I was dead wrong about in my youth was in thinking that I didn't need friendships. I thought, *"I don't need that. I'm independent, big deal!"* That's probably a bit different than many women felt during their younger years, when being surrounded by a lot of friends seemed to be the norm. But for me, I had my own set of friends from so long ago, that I felt I didn't need to add another one. Since I've been in my forties, I've found that relationships help to ease other issues that you may have, and you need somebody to just bounce things off of. Sharing your thoughts and feelings allows you to feel better about your relationships with your children, your mate, and helps with other issues as well. You need those girlfriends to laugh with, and cry with. In my twenties and thirties, females were always considered my competition, so I didn't want to be around too many of them. Now I look at other women as a reflection of myself. *"Hmmm, is that something I would wear, or is that something I would say..."*

I look for desirable attributes in women that I may want to emulate in my own life, and I check myself on the undesirable attributes to make sure I'm not behaving in a similar way. Young women are always comparing themselves to each other and it's primarily about men, *"Do I have the best car? Do I have the best body?"* So it's very liberating to be free of the competitive mindset.

"FORTIES IS A MUCH CALMER TIME FOR ME. I HAVE THE SELF-CONFIDENCE AND THE WISDOM TO DISTINGUISH BETWEEN WHAT'S IMPORTANT AND WHAT'S NOT, AND NOW REALIZE THE UNIMPORTANT THINGS DON'T REALLY MATTER."

It's also liberating to know the truth about men, they're not all that! I should have had a DNA test kit with me at all times. In fact, I want to advise young women to seriously consider some type of DNA testing on men to determine their genetic makeup. Stop looking at him for who he is now, because all that will fade. Instead, try to determine who he is going to be as you continue on in life together, because he's going to turn forty as well. I love my husband, but I realize now that I don't have to have a man. It's not about the sex, but it's more about having a mutually rewarding relationship.

I remember being younger and out with my girls, and the qualifier was always, *"Oooh girl, he is cute!"* We didn't realize "cute" was going to get old, his hair was going to grey, his belly was going to bulge and all that other stuff was going to go too. Sometimes, when you're trying to communicate and you're sitting up attempting to have a Barack Obama conversation, it's just not happening. You should try and wait until you're forty to have a relationship, because you'll appreciate what matters more then, and hopefully, find a man who can fulfill you intellectually. You might want to find out what the last book was that he read.

And, wow! What faulty thinking I had in my youth, almost to the point of regret. I had goals for what I wanted to do or become, and they were constantly changing. One of them was to get my master's degree, but I didn't have a plan for what to do with that degree. I just said, *"Get a master's degree,"* which I was able to accomplish before I was forty. If only I paid attention to those things back in my twenties, even before graduating from college, I probably would have stayed in school and pursued my master's and doctorate in succession, but I failed to think it through. My primary goal back then was to just hurry up and get the degree, without ever really thinking that one day I would turn forty or fifty and know what my long term goals were.

I was very impatient and somewhat strong willed in my youth, and really determined to do it my way. Forties is a much calmer time for me. I have the self-confidence and the wisdom to distinguish between what's important and what's not, and now realize that the unimportant things don't really matter. I was on a trip this weekend along with another younger teacher, and she wanted to know, *"What keeps you so calm? Why don't any of these things bother you?"* It's because I've been there... running off at the mouth, I replied, *"Hurry up and do this, hurry up and do that"* and *"You can't tell me!"* Now, I can just sit back, calmly observe and watch what's going to happen. It's a mellowing of the mind that takes place and you realize you shouldn't take things as seriously. There is no fear that the world is going to end and I had better hurry up and get some of this before it's gone. Even as I supervise people, there is a calmness I now enjoy that has come with age.

That newfound tranquility also comes in handy when I'm looking at my body these days. I'm embracing my body so much better now than I did twenty or twenty five years ago. When I was younger, I obsessed over my body, even though I didn't have to. As far as I'm concerned, just being young makes you beautiful; the dewy cheeks, the fluttering eyelashes and the ripe breasts. It's a beautiful thing!

I've been fortunate in the face, and that's probably due to good genes. I haven't seen a major change in my face as I've grown older, and even other people find it difficult to guess my age. But it's when I take my clothes off that I know there's a difference. Thank God for Spanx, and places like QVC, that will introduce you to a full line of body shapers that can help you bring that youthful figure back. Anything that will suck it in or hold it in, they made it for me! I was used to having a pouch in my stomach, but I could make it disappear when I needed it to. Going through early menopause has made the pouch even more noticeable and it's the body shapers that help me maintain my figure now. And can somebody please tell me what's going on with my butt? I never really had any hips, but my butt was always nice and round, like an apple. Now it looks like there's something at the top and nothing underneath. It's almost like there's a knot or a bump, and then there's a flat part that was not there before and I'm wondering, *"What in the world happened to my butt? Am I sitting too much or something?"*

I have become an avid reader of fashion literature and I make sure to wear clothing that's going to flatter my body. I wear the best bras, because the girls are not going to sit up by themselves anymore. And even with a good bra, I may have to go in and lift them up in the afternoon, because they get tired after lunch and they fall. I am very comfortable with my body, and I honor my body by dressing in a manner that compliments it. At first there was a little shock when I started to notice some changes. I looked in the mirror one day and thought, *"Lord, what happened?"* I now know what to expect when I get up in the morning. I bought a subscription to Lucky magazine, and it gives me all the tips and tricks I need to address my changing body.

I know that nothing is certain and life is fleeting. When I received the news about my mother's breast cancer, I was of course, devastated. But because of the timing in my life I was able to recover very quickly. Had I still been in my twenties or thirties when this happened, I would likely still be grieving, even though my mother is very much alive.

After forty, you're in the second half of life; you realize you're not going to live forever and you know you have to make the most of it. I make the most of each day and I reflect every evening, *"Was today okay? Did I do things right today?"*

BRENDA POLLARD

I talk to my mother just about every day now. My son was born with neurofibromatosis. In my twenties and thirties, I never allowed myself to think about it. In my forties, when he began to go through puberty, the neurofibromatosis began to grow. As his hormones changed, the condition became more prominent, and now he has a growth the size of a baseball in his elbow. Now, instead of just listening to doctors, I do my own research and I'm teaching him that his condition doesn't change anything; *"You're going to play your instrument, you're going to grow up and get married, you're going to make a decision about whether or not you want to have children,"* nothing has changed. This is the maturity and the wisdom I have acquired now, that I lacked before. And because of my forty plus and fabulous attitude, my teenage son has a very positive outlook and is handling his condition very well. That means everything to me.

WHAT GOLDEN NUGGETS DID YOU GET FROM THIS TREASURE CHEST OF WISDOM?

AJ

Boutique Owner and Stylist, Jamali Fashion and Accessories

Age 58

It's interesting that so many women approach their forties with feelings of fright. They think after thirty, life is over. But I'm here to tell you, at forty, life begins. At fifty, it gets even better; and I'm heading towards sixty and getting even more excited about it!

There are a couple of things that women go through as we age, and for a very long time, especially in the black community, women didn't talk about these things. You're going to experience a few unpleasant moments from time to time. Hot flashes are one of them, but that doesn't mean it's not exciting! Just get yourself a cute little battery operated fan and go on about your business.

I will be fifty eight this year and I work very hard. I know I can't prevent getting older, but I don't have to be old and fat! So many women just let themselves go, and you don't want to do that, ladies.

I sell clothing for women ages thirty and up, and I don't offer anything in my boutique for young people. Just because you reach forty plus doesn't mean you have to look forty plus, at least not in the old fashioned stereotypical way. I tell people all the time, *"When I'm in my eighties, I'm going to be so sharp that people are going to say, 'Look at AJ, still looking young.'"*

For me, I love to be seen so, I may be a little more flamboyant than other women choose to be, but still, I'm not to the point where I'm outrageous. I like a showy, sassy, chic look. Some women go a little overboard, but my job is to try and bring them back from the wild side. Then, you have some who understate their beauty. They don't know quite how to dress, or how to get the right fit or select the right style or color. I talk to so many women, particularly women ages fifty and up, who once were told that only whores wore red. But you can also be a whore wearing black, blue, green or purple. Red is a beautiful color. For a woman who has a vibrant attitude, is very energetic and ambitious, red is a great color for her. It's a power color! It lets the world know you are confident and feel good about who you are.

That's why I love being over forty. I enjoy that sense of confidence. I say what I mean and I do what I say I'm going to do. It's a wonderful way of living life. You go through all the changes of being in your twenties and thirties, but for me, my fifties are absolutely wonderful. I enjoy being a woman and feeling good everyday. I take good care of myself. I workout when I am home. Three years ago, I lost thirty-five pounds and went from a size 12 to a size 8, and I feel great. I had energy all along, but now I feel even more active and alive. Sometimes, it's hard for me to stop and realize it's time to shut it down, because I'm so ambitious. I'm one of those women who want to make sure every "I" is dotted and every "T" is crossed; I strive for perfection constantly.

I love the Lord and I'm a true child of God, but I don't feel like you have to carry a bible or preach to people. The way you carry yourself and the way you treat others will be a reflection of the God in you.

There is nothing I miss about my youth, but there are things I wish I could go back to, knowing what I know now, and do over. There are definitely a few things I would do differently. How many times do we say to ourselves,*"If I had known then what I know now?"* But, I don't have any regrets. I lost my parents at a very young age, so I had to raise sisters and brothers, which means I've been grown up for a long time. I've been very mature for a long time. Life is something you have to live every single day as if it is your last day.

In 2001, my husband gave me a surprise birthday party on December 14th. On December 18th, he had a massive heart attack and died. I've lost a lot of family members in my lifetime, at a very early age, and it's given me a deeper appreciation for life. With me, what you see is what you get, and I tell people, *"If you don't want the truth, don't ask me!"*

My name is Alice, and I have created an acronym from the initial letters; A= *Ambitious*, L= *Loveable*, I = *Intelligent*, C = *Charming*, and E = *Exciting*. This is the place I have come to with maturing. Pre-forty was not a very exciting time for me. As I said earlier, my parents died at a very early age, so I was raising sisters and brothers. I was caught in a place where I did not

"BE CLOSE TO THE SAME AGE, BECAUSE YOUR BODY IS GOING TO CHANGE. WHEN IT HAPPENS— DON'T FRET; JUST GET YOURSELF SOME SPANX OR BODY SHAPERS, AND WORK WITH WHAT YOU'VE GOT! "

want to be, but I had to do it because my father died of a massive heart attack in 1980, and my mother died in 1982 of lung cancer. I gave up my job in order to have that time to be with my mom. I made a promise that I would be there, not only for my sisters and brothers, but also for my mother's mother who was still alive at the time. I was thrust into a situation where I had a lot of responsibility. I was no longer in a place where I was free and single. I couldn't travel and do what I wanted when and how I wanted. All of that was suddenly shut down.

I had my own son late in life, at the age of forty-one. He is sixteen years old now, and I love him with everything I have. But again, I'm sort of stuck in a place. I don't regret it. I'm still not able to do a lot of the things I want to do, but I only have two more years to go and I shall be free!

I enjoy being single but I've noticed a lot of women, especially if they're not married or have never been, go through this "funk" stage somewhere between thirty and forty. They look at themselves as getting old, but they don't realize that the rainbow is on the other side of turning forty, and it's wonderful. If you're together mentally, spiritually and physically, I'm telling you, the sky is the limit!

I think many men over fifty want a younger woman because they're trying to revitalize themselves, but it's a mistake. God says we must be equally yoked, and He meant that in every stage of life. If I'm fifty, you need to be fifty too because if I have a pain, you can understand that pain because you're experiencing the same type of thing yourself. But if I'm having a pain and I've got me a "YTM" (Young, Tender, Morsel) he's not going to understand what I'm going through. A lot of older women now are dating younger men, I think they call them "cougars," and that's fine if they want to. But I want someone on the same intellectual level I'm on, who likes the music I like and enjoys the same things that I do. If my arthritis in my arm is bothering me, I don't want to hear anyone say, *"Well, every time I turn around, your arm is bothering you!"* If he's fifty-something, like me, his leg might be hurting or he might have a bad knee. We can understand each others pain and suffering.

Haven't you known couples where one may have come from a one parent home, while the other came from a two parent home, and the person from the one parent home became very jealous of the relationship the spouse has with their parents? That happened to me! I've been married twice, and my first husband came from a single parent home. My parents and I were very, very close. No matter where I lived, they would come to visit with me, and my husband would get very upset, *"Why are they always coming to see you? Why do they have to come this weekend?"* Finally I had to tell him, *"Look, my parents are John and Shirley Johnson and you might as well go sit on the bench, outside, take a trip, I don't care! But they are coming!"* He didn't understand that. If I had married someone who also had two parents, it probably would not have been such a problem for him. He would have understood the closeness of family.

Granted, there are some exceptions to every rule, but for the majority, it can present some real challenges. Be close to the same age because your body is going to change. When it happens—don't fret; just get yourself some Spanx or body shapers, and work with what you've got! I wear them myself. My body is not perfect. Gravity takes over. Maya Angelou made a remark on Oprah Winfrey one day that she didn't know which one of her breasts were trying to get to her waist first. It happens.

This doesn't just pertain to women, it happens to men as well. But a fifty year old man can't talk about your body because his body is sagging too. So I tell women, *"Whatever you have to do to fit into that dress and look neat, do it!"* Do whatever is necessary to feel good about yourself.

It was after I turned forty that I started my own business. I believe "it ain't over, 'til it's over," and that's when you're six feet under! Nothing is impossible unless you make it impossible. I had a dream of owning my own business. I went to Florida and attended A&M University and earned a degree in Marketing. I worked in corporate America in sales for 10 years. The thing that was so disgusting for me, especially during that era, was that people judged you by the color of your skin, not by your abilities. In a lot of cases, black women were the last ones, in some industries, to get promoted. In the industry I was in, they promoted a few black men in higher positions, and then it was the white female, followed by the black female. But the thing that really got to me was feeling like I wasn't making what I was worth, because I knew that I had the abilities.

My 87 year old grandmother, bless her heart, asked me when I told her I was going to open my business, *"What are you going to do that for? How are you going to do it?"* She also added a lot more negative input. Now, I could have listened to her and she could have gotten me to a point where I doubted myself, but I knew what I could do, and I wouldn't allow her to discourage me. If I could make money for someone else, I could surely make money for myself.

I tell people to find your niche, and work as hard for yourself, as you worked for someone else! Women have got to take it upon themselves to build up enough confidence and step out on faith. Don't let anyone tell you what you can't do.

WHAT GOLDEN NUGGETS DID YOU GET FROM THIS
TREASURE CHEST OF WISDOM?

_____

_____

_____

_____

_____

_____

_____

_____

_____

_____

_____

_____

_____

NANCY CRANBOURNE

Choreographer and Director, 40 Women Over 40 Dance Troup
Age 53

I've been dancing professionally and doing theater since I was 22, and it felt like I was finding my way the whole time. I remember my fortieth birthday. My husband and I were at a beach called Cannon Beach in Oregon. I will never forget that day, because the water was really cold and no one dared to go in. But we decided we needed to, because it was my birthday, and we were treating it almost like a christening celebration

We were running around in a circle in the water, screaming because it was so cold, and people on the beach were asking, *"Are you guys okay? Are you alright?"* and we just smiled back and shouted, *"Yeah, we're fine!"* My husband was really handsome back then. He was wearing a blue bathing suit, and we were running and laughing together on the beach and it felt very liberating. When I turned forty, I felt like, *"Okay, this is it! You have got to really do what you want the way you want it now. You can't blame your mother anymore; you can't blame your upbringing. You gotta grow up, really!"*

Before I turned forty, I was a real people pleaser and got by with using a lot of charm. In my family, my brother was very intense, as was my father, while my mom remained indifferent. As a little girl, I became the peace-maker, *"Everybody calm down and let's just chill!"* I was taught to be delightful and not make waves. I rode on that for a long, long time, wanting people to like me and never argued with anyone.

I really didn't come into my own true being until I was in my forties. I felt that I was now able to cut through things with a big sword. I'm very clear on boundaries, very clear on relationships, and really listen to my heart, rather than being led by "shoulds." Now, instead of saying, *"I should do this, I gotta do that,"* I say, *"I am able to do this, I want to do that, and this is what I'm doing."* It's absolutely up to me to choose who I'm with and where I want to be, and I'm completely led by the soul, rather than by the brain.

"TOO MANY WOMEN BELIEVE THE ADVERTISING CULTURE IN THIS COUNTRY, AND IT'S TIME FOR US TO TAKE OUR POWER BACK AND DECLARE, 'YOU KNOW WHAT, WE ARE QUEENS! WE ARE TRUE GODDESSES!' AND, DON'T TAKE ANY BULLSHIT!"

In all the male paradigms of how you view the world, it's got to be logical, you've got to work it out and you've got to think it through. Now I can just deeply listen to my heart and soul and know exactly what I'm doing and it's never led me astray. I really started honing that after I turned forty, and that was a huge change from when I was a little girl, compared to the woman I've become.

I think that our culture really does a disservice to women over forty; they still do in all the magazines. *MORE* magazine is still showing skinny, completely anorexic actresses as examples of beauty, and it's supposed to be a magazine for women over forty. I want to shout, *"Mix it up more!"*

Don't keep being tyrannical with your expectations of everyone else. I read that magazine and I thought, *"Really? You guys still believe that line that you've got to look like that to be okay?"* As a dancer all these years, if you're deeply in your body, you know you don't have to look like that to be gorgeous, and sexy and desirable. I was telling my class today, *"Just walk down the street."* I've been doing this experiment a lot, where I walk down the street very slowly. I'm in my body, and I'm really loving my woman's body, and I walk and just see what the energy is like around me. If you just own it and you're walking in it, the energy surrounding you is really invigorating. Try walking slowly, and owning your body when you're out. Try it for 10 minutes in the grocery store, and see what happens!

Too many women believe the advertising culture in this country, and it's time for us to take our power back and declare, *"You know what, we are queens! We are true goddesses!"* And don't take any bullshit!

I want to give the ladies in my dance troupe what I've gotten, which I consider is a gift. I've honed it, I've worked on it, but it's also a gift that was given to me and I felt like this since I was a child. I was always sort of a wild and wonderful kid, and I was allowed to be me. My parents were very loving, and they allowed me to run wild outdoors and in the woods. I was a tomboy when I was younger, and could climb trees, peel the bark, pet animals and roll around in the grass, feeling the warmth of the sun on my body. I looked like a little Aborigine back then. As I started growing up, that part of me became more oppressed by my mother's insistence that I wear Ann Taylor suits and look conservative in order to attract a certain type of husband. I was probably twelve or thirteen years old at the time, and looked at her in disbelief and said, *"Are you kidding me? That's never going to be who I am!"* That's not what I'm supposed to be. That's not what God, or the Source, or Buddah, or whoever you believe in, wants from me! It wants me to keep honing that wild child into this really moving, sensual, powerful, fierce human being. And so for me, I now own that; I own my body and I own the expression of these things.

So what I want to impart to these women is to have them use their own power, and their own expression and have them take back ownership of their bodies. Women need to stop comparing themselves to other people too. We've been through a lot to get to where we are now, and we've earned our spot. I want to give them that freedom too. When you're training dancers, you're training them to have the technique, which is the beginning of the foundation, and it's like building a house. Then you decorate it beautifully, which is the expression over the technique. This is my true calling; to bring as many women as I can forward though this process of dance. I have dancers in my company who are much better dancers than I am. They're doing my choreography, and its like, *"Wow!"* You're having a dream come true right in front of you. So it's time to give them back themselves, and that is what I'm really trying to do.

I had a really great childhood, but there's nothing about my youth that I miss. It's really my time now to crack open the Universe and do the most courageous thing I can do. I've learned to say "no" really well, and saying "no" has been a huge accomplishment for me. I take really good care of myself, and when I start to feel tired or I start to get sick, I take all my remedies; a hot bath, watch a movie, go to bed and cancel everything. I don't push through stuff like I used to, I really listen to what's going on deep within my body.

Women should just go for it and go for it big! Just do everything you can do and whatever it is that you want to do. It's really the only path to take, and the Universe will support you for it. It will get the people you need in life and guide you where you need to go. The final result will be amazing, if you're willing to just take that first step. Go for what scares the hell out of you! I promise you that if you do, it will be a satisfying journey.

WHAT GOLDEN NUGGETS DID YOU GET FROM THIS TREASURE CHEST OF WISDOM?

_____

_____

_____

_____

_____

YANA BERLIN

Founder, Fabulously40.com
Age 44

I think that forty and beyond are the best years of our life. When we're in our twenties we're still kids and we're trying to figure out what life is all about. At thirty, women are usually busy with family, kids, and PTA. But when we approach forty, we come into our own and we finally figure out who we are and what we want. At the same time, we're still young, so we can basically discover what it is that makes us happy, what it is that makes us tick, and capitalize on that. We are not as shy or timid as we were in our twenties and thirties, and we can now do what we wanted to do but weren't able to do until we got our voice.

Almost four years ago now, I was turning forty and, I had a really great support group of girlfriends. We've been friends for thirty years and these are the girls I can also bounce ideas off; get support whether for fun, or for something serious. Well, around the same time I was getting calls; a couple of them were unhappy, some were talking about getting a divorce, and I couldn't understand what the heck was going on.

It was kind of the same thing from everyone and we now have this rule that only one of us can get crazy at a time. So when I saw a couple of them getting wacky I said, *"Okay, emergency weekend in Palm Springs!"* We all went to Palm Springs, and basically when I got them all together in the room, I found out that half of them were not happy with what they had. They were not happy with their husbands, or their kids, or their parents. As I was listening, one of them said, *"I can't be married to my husband, he is cheap."* and I said, *"Well, he was cheap twenty-five years ago, but remember, you were the one who wanted to marry him, not us. So, what happened?"* She says, *"Well I can't take it anymore!"*

So I spent the weekend listening to what everyone had to say, and when I returned from Palm Springs, I had this epiphany. It wasn't everyone else who had changed; it was *we* who had changed. We don't want to do the same things we wanted to do twenty years ago. We have our own voice now. I have a girlfriend who was always so quiet, and then all of a sudden she had an opinion about everything. So of course, now her husband is pissed off, her kids are pissed off, because she never said anything all her life, and now she wants it her way! I came back and I said to my husband, *"You know, this is great, but at the same time, how are we going to work through this? What if I were to go nuts like this in the next year or two?"*

I went to sleep that night thinking about this whole thing. I had two kids on My Space, two kids on Facebook, and I woke up at three o'clock in the morning with this idea—*"What about Fabulously 40?"* I woke my husband at 3:00 a.m. and said, *"What about Fabulously 40?"* He looked at me like I was delusional. He thought, this was the time I had lost it, you know? We just had this conversation four hours ago, and here I am, before the sun can even come up, with this idea. He said, *"What about it?"* and I say, *"Well, what if I create a space for women where they can share and connect, they're in the same demographics and everybody is going through the same challenges. It's just a big group of women to drive, share, connect and have fun"* and he goes, *"That's a fabulous idea! Now go write a business plan."* He actually made me get up at three o'clock in the morning and write a business plan. I think he just wanted to get rid of me because he wanted to go back to sleep. But that's exactly what I did. We started the website and it kind of evolved.

Because of that special demographic, because of that special age, we can all relate to one another. We might come from different walks of life, we might have different religions and races, but we all have one thing in common. It's about those changes, physical changes, and psychological changes that happen during that age.

I really believe it's the girlfriends in our life who move us forward. I have a great husband, who is very supportive and very caring, and I have wonderful children. But my inspiration and my encouragement come mostly from my girlfriends. They think that I can do it, and if they think I can do it—I think I can do it too. They can relate to me more so than my husband or my children can, because they're going through the same changes I'm going through. When I'm talking to my girlfriends about my PMS, I don't have to explain to them, *"I'm being a bitch today because of my PMS."* It's the other people in our lives that we have to explain things to, but with our girlfriends, it's so easy. That's why every time I get together with my group I'm recharged. All my kids love it when I go away with the girls. I come back as a better person and a better mom. I'm so much saner. That is the power of having girlfriends.

"WOMEN OVER FORTY SHOULD SEE THEMSELVES AS VERY MARKETABLE. AGE IS JUST A NUMBER, AND I CAN ASSURE YOU, IF I WANTED TO GET A JOB RIGHT NOW I COULD WALK INTO A COMPANY, IF I'M QUALIFIED, AND GET THE JOB."

Don't fight the physical changes, because I don't. If somebody wants plastic surgery, whatever they want to do to feel good about themselves, I'm all for it! I just personally never thought, that for me, having a boob job was something I would ever want to do. I woke up one morning and I'm standing there, butt naked in front of my bed. My boobs are hanging down somewhere below my knees, my husband is brushing his teeth and I come up to him and say, *"You know, maybe I should have a boob lift!"* He looked at me and he says to me, *"Why would you do that?"* I said, *"Well honey, when gravity takes its toll, things sag."* And he says, *"Well, when they sag, we'll talk about it!"* I looked at him and said, *"You're absolutely right."* I took one boob and threw it over one shoulder, and took the other boob and threw it over the other shoulder and said, *"We'll never talk about this again."* You know, if he thinks they're not sagging, I'm good with that. The reason he responded that way was because I never talked about it before. I always accepted me for the way I am. There was a time when I wanted to be skinny, but I never could. I was born at 150, 160 lbs. and I'll probably die this way. There's nothing I can do to get rid of the weight, unless I get sick, and I don't want to get sick. The thing is, we have to embrace ourselves. We have to say to ourselves, *"Look, this is me, and I love me for who I am!"*

Most people see us for the way we see ourselves. I never thought I would need any kind of lift or surgery; I never projected that. Nobody ever thought I needed to lose weight. But if I start saying right now, *"Oh I need to lose weight, I'm fat..,"* guess what's going to happen? Everyone in my family is going to think that way too, because it's what we project on ourselves and other people. Love yourselves. If you have a butt, great, embrace it! Being forty, fifty or sixty, it's not about how you look; it's about how you feel that makes you look the way you do. I have a family doctor who is about fifty pounds overweight and let me tell you, she is one of the happiest people I know. I met a woman one day, a couple of months ago, and she's a twig. We went to lunch and she eats like she's eating for three men. I looked at her and I said, *"Honey, you and I could never be close, because sitting next to you I could get really fat."* She loves food, but she's not happy. She is trapped in this tiny body, whereas the doctor friend of mine is a big girl, she loves life and she laughs and it's so great to see. It doesn't matter how small or big your waist is, or how flat your stomach is. At forty-five, unless you're in the physical fitness field, how fit can you be? We do our best, but if anybody wants to check me for muscle resistance, I would not be a good candidate. Accept yourself and move on. Concentrate on other things that are so much more important.

Women over forty should see themselves as very marketable. Age is just a number, and I can assure you, if I wanted to get a job right now I could walk into a company, if I'm qualified, and get the job. Again, it's the projections we have. I'm a business person and I would rather hire someone who is forty, forty-five, or fifty, rather than hire a twenty-five or thirty-year old. I'll tell you why—I have kids, and I remember what kind of hell it was trying to figure out what you do with one child who is sick, one who looks like he may be getting sick, and another you need to take to school; it's that juggling act we do when we're moms.

Women over forty are so much more focused on what they're doing. What we have to do as women over forty is to stay current with the times. We have to be in tune and stay on top of things that are going on. If you're a woman over forty and you're applying for a job, but you've never heard of Twitter or don't know how to create an Excel spreadsheet, you may not get the job. Not because you're over forty, but because you're not current with the times; this is the information age and we have to keep up with technology.

I just did a blog with David Matthews, who writes a column from the male perspective. It's basically about what men find sexy in a woman, and what women think men find sexy in a woman. I think it's all about confidence. But first, we really have to be happy with who we are. When we're happy and confident and when we get our groove back, we can have anyone and we can do anything.

Most men are very insecure, and they gravitate towards women who are confident. In general, people want to be around happy people. But dating is never easy, right? Do you remember dating in your twenties? Was that fun? The only problem I have with dating today is having a relationship over Skype, or breaking up over a text message or Blackberry messaging. If I were dating today, I would want to have the same thing I had thirty years ago. I want to be courted. I want to be picked up. I want to be taken out to dinner. I don't want this message on my phone, *"Hi, I had a good time."* Bologna! Call me and tell me you had a good time, and send me flowers. A friend of mine had been dating for a while, and resorted to this texting, Blackberry messaging, emailing, and Skype. She had her heart broken a couple of times. I finally said to her, *"You know what, you are putting yourself out there and you're telling them it is okay. The next time you meet a guy, you tell him it is not okay!"*

So, the next time she went on a date, the guy asked her if she had a Blackberry. She said, *"Yes, I have a Blackberry, but I don't do anything over the phone; no text messaging, no BBM'ing. If you want to talk to me, you call me."* They've been dating for a couple of months now and it's going great. If you tell a man you are old fashioned, and old fashioned nowadays means you're not going to text and have a relationship over the phone, he will respect that.

When I hear women moaning about turning forty or approaching midlife, I want them to know that it's the best age. I don't know about you, but I would not want to be twenty again, or thirty, for that matter. If I could stay forty or forty-five, I'd be great. But even at fifty or sixty, if you're taking care of yourself, you will be fine. If you're happy, everything else will just fall into place. Open your mind, embrace what you have, and figure out what it is that you excel in. We cannot excel at everything, but we all have special gifts. There is something in you and something in me, and something in another woman that is very unique. If we can just tune into that; if we can find out what is unique and what makes us tick—that is what we should concentrate on. That is what is going to make us happy. Whether it's building a business or having a hobby, do something just for you and nourish your soul.

Approaching forty is good, but approaching eighty is even better. As long as we keep getting older, we're doing great; and if we can do it with a smile on our face, we've solved that problem called "life."

WHAT GOLDEN NUGGETS DID YOU GET FROM THIS TREASURE CHEST OF WISDOM?

EVA LaRUE

Former Miss California Empire, Model, Actress (*All My Children, CSI: Miami*)

Age 44

Recognizing the value of the over forty woman is long overdue. I would say, ten years ago, before the advent of *Desperate Housewives* and *Sex in the City*, the only thing that was in was to be twenty-five, and all the people that were working were just these young hot girls. There were just so few women in their forties who were considered "hot," or who were considered sexy or marketable. Now, there's this whole group of women who are really beautiful, sexy and marketable women. There's Halle Berry, J-Lo, Terry Hatcher and many more. All of these women are thirty-nine or forty and it's exciting. It used to be only Susan Sarandon; she was the only hot mama actress, so it's really exciting now to see that even in their forties these women are still considered hot and still considered beautiful.

"PRE-FORTY EVA SWEATED THE SMALL STUFF FAR TOO MUCH, LIVED LIFE A LITTLE MORE BLACK AND WHITE, AND OBSESSED OVER STUFF THAT WAS REALLY NOT WORTH IT. I'M NO LONGER AS JUDGMENTAL OF MYSELF."

I have to say, I actually got really lucky and have good genes. My mom and dad both still look really young. My dad is seventy-four, and you would never think it. He has that great Puerto Rican skin that ages beautifully, and I am lucky to have a lot of that too. My body has changed a lot from my twenties to my forties and, for a while there, I had put on an extra twenty pounds. I think if I had done that in my twenties, I would have had a heart attack or just thrown myself from the nearest building. But it's funny, when you're in your thirties you're like, *"Oh, these are my war wounds from being pregnant,"* and you just start to accept yourself more.

Then, I started to pull it together and I got back in shape. I lost twenty pounds, and I actually feel like I have a better body now than I did when I was twenty. When you're in your twenties you totally obsess over your body. You don't appreciate it at all, and once you get into your thirties, you start to get a little more lax with yourself. By the time you're forty, I think you find a nice balance between not obsessing, but certainly having to work harder to keep your body together, and appreciating what your body looks like.

Pre-forty Eva sweated the small stuff far too much, lived life a little more black and white, and obsessed over stuff that was really not worth it. I'm no longer as judgmental of myself. By the time you're past your thirties, you begin to see an emotionally softer side of yourself. You realize there is no black or white, and you're living more in a grey area. You're certainly more accepting of other people's perspectives, and I think it makes life easier. You enjoy things a lot more; you appreciate things a lot more, because you've worked hard to get them.

My life is so full, that I only try to keep people around me whom I really love, and who really enhance my life. We spend so much wasted time in our twenties and thirties, allowing people to steal our time; people who want to suck from your life, but not give anything back. By the time I turned forty, I had an entirely different perspective and thought, *"Wow, life's too short and I don't want to hang out with you!"*

For me, life definitely began in my forties. I feel like I had so much figuring out to do. When I was in my twenties, I thought that by the time you reached forty the end was near. Now I think there are so many people who are proving that theory wrong. After forty, you know what you're looking for and relationships can improve.

My sister, who is not forty yet, just went back to college two years ago and she's getting ready to graduate this summer. She's three years younger than I am and wants to become a school teacher. In addition to attending college, she loves to bake and was supporting herself through school by working as a waitress.

She started making all the desserts for the restaurant where she works. Then they opened a second restaurant, and she started making desserts for that one too. This created a whole side business for her that she never planned. Up until then, her ambition was to become a school teacher. She is now making money with a baking business, and is able to support herself with it. It's never too late for a woman to live her dreams. There's a whole future in front of you. With the way the stock market fluctuates and the recessed economy, I think we're all going to be working a whole hell-of-a-lot longer than we thought we were going to! I don't think retirement is going to come anytime soon. So if you have to reinvent yourself to support your life, explore every area, because you never know what you will find, or what opportunity is out there waiting for you.

WHAT GOLDEN NUGGETS DID YOU GET FROM THIS
TREASURE CHEST OF WISDOM?

_____

_____

_____

_____

_____

_____

_____

_____

_____

_____

_____

_____

SUE TAYLOR

Legal Professional
Age 50

Oh, heck yeah! I'm soon to be 50 and I absolutely LOVE my age. I love my grey hairs coming through. I love every line in my face. I love that I'm a Nanna to the dearest little souls. I love that I'm so much better than I was at 25. I love knowing that these truly are my very best years. I am indeed loving every bit of it!

When my adult alpha male friends, leading independent lives; totally not needing mommy, call me up just to ask me what I think of things because they respect my opinion—that's amazing. It's not possible to have that at twenty-five. There are so many things you can only understand when you're that age. If you're twenty years old and you're hot, you're getting attention and people are flocking to you. When you're fifty and you don't have all of that, you're not that little beauty anymore, who are you and what are you? You better be fabulous, because when you're fabulous, it doesn't matter. You've still got it! You've still got those twenty year olds looking up to you; you've still got those people flocking to

"WHEN YOU'RE TWENTY, YOU DON'T REALIZE WHAT TOXIC IS AND WHAT TOXIC CAN DO TO YOU. AND FACE IT, SOME PEOPLE ARE JUST TOXIC."

you. You're still attracting, but it's so much better. Now you're attracting a far more meaningful life; it's not just frivolity.

If you're trapped by your peer's opinions, you're in trouble; but, by this age we now know better. We know what we want; we know how to get what we want, we know how to attract what we want and how to pass those blessings on to others. I've never met a twenty year old in my life who could say that.

Would I ever want to be twenty again, heck no! Are you kidding me? When you're twenty, you don't realize what toxic is and what it can do to you. And face it, some people are just toxic. Those people can change the entire course of your life without you even realizing it. But at this time of life, for most of us anyway, you're quicker to speak up for yourself because you have that wisdom, you have that knowing and you won't tolerate it. And I don't give a little rats honey how really fantastic it looks superficially—if it's toxic—I'm outta there! The last guy I dated found that out.

The man I was with was incredibly important to me. I adored him. He is into natural health, a Shiatsu Therapist and Qigong instructor, handsome, witty, a lovely man on the surface—but a cripple beneath - always blaming others for his poor little lot in life, which really isn't that bad. He's happy, seemingly for a few days, and then he drones on for days about past nonsense and can't seem (more like - doesn't want) to just get over himself and past all the junk. I've known him for a few years and found him delightful. I had never seen the *other* side. I moved in with him, at his persuasion, last November 1st. We attended a wedding together that night with mutual friends, and we had a very good thing for a very short time. He soon became very toxic. I saw behaviors that I knew were not in my best interest to partner up with. By the 1st of February this year, I was outta' there! He was shocked and asked me to stay, but no dice! Right after Christmas and New Year's, I told him I was leaving and began to make my arrangements. I told him I would be gone by the 15th of January.

On January 14th, only one day before I was to move, my father died. How horrific do you suppose that was? Now I was losing the two most important men in my life all at once, and within only two weeks of each other. I had to put my moving plans on hold, which meant I remained in that situation until I could take care of my family's needs which required top priority. I had to go back home to bury my father, then return and deal with the next load of grief on my home front. I had to round up my three boys, schedule everyone together, contact my extended family members, help with funeral arrangements and deal with my tremendously grievous home front. It took a couple of days to get everyone in sync. My boys all have professions that require varying schedules, and so do I. I was dealing with the most horrific grief I've ever experienced, while still having to be in a place I so desperately wanted to leave. So what to do?

I went to my father's house, put on his comfy old pajamas, climbed into his bed, snuggled into his pillows and cried my little heart out all night long. But all the while, my self-talk was keeping me on track. I was so grieved. I thought *"What on earth does a daddy's girl do without a daddy? How will I ever get used to being without him?"* But then I got a hold of myself and kept telling myself—no matter what, I'm going to be okay. I will not lean on that guy who I fully intend to leave when I get back there. I will not allow my grief to become a stumbling block, or to impede me in what I know is the best thing for me to do. I just kept talking myself through it all.

At age 20, I would have sought all the comfort from that guy that I could get. My grief would have been just the crutch I needed, and I would have stayed in a bad thing, only to have to face the reality sooner or later. At my age, I know how to approach life from a position of strength and independence. And that's what I did. I returned from the funeral and was gone from that situation in less than two weeks' time. No matter how much I miss or love him, I have restrained myself from making a single phone call. I absolutely refuse to get myself re-entangled!

I am now in the place I want to be. I am in the neighborhood I've wanted to be in, and I'm incredibly happy in my life; and it all happened in a short time because I know, at this age, what is best for me and how to stick to my guns to achieve it! Even under the most horrific circumstances, I flat out refuse to surrender to anyone or anything that goes against my better judgment. I'm not wasting my fabulous, my good years, on nonsense.

One of the greatest things I've ever done for myself was to give myself permission to just be. I don't have to be anything in particular; I just have to be me. At twenty you don't realize that. You think you have to be what you see on TV, what you read in magazines, and what your peers tell you. At forty, the lights go on and you realize it's just a bunch of junk. You are what you eat, and I don't eat that junk.

I don't sit around pining about how alone I am. You think just because there's no one around that I'm alone? That's craziness! That presence that's in this Universe, is always with me. The global insanity we're taught since childhood would have me think I'm alone, but I don't feed from that troth.

After forty, you figure out where your spot is in life. Your instincts are keener, and you know what is and isn't a good place for you. So when I've made up my mind that something is right for me, I listen to no one. If I know that it's something I could have, and something I should have, and it's a good spot for me to move into, there is nothing that's going to stop me. I'm going to do it, I'm telling you now, and I'd like to see the person who is going to stop me.

I really don't care that I have to go through the physical symptoms of aging. It is part of my biological life so, why not just embrace it? Is it a pain in the neck? Heck, yeah! But so are half the things we do. Is it a joy to maintain your car? Well sometimes it's not a joy to maintain your body either. Does it make the car a bad thing? No. Does it make your body a bad thing? No. Who in their right mind loves a really good hot flash? But here again, it just is. And it's really a great time too. It's all part of becoming you. I certainly have compassion for any woman who is experiencing extreme symptoms, but it's so great that we have alternatives our mothers never had.

I was just reading in *BBC Published*, the absolutely shocking stats on the number of women over forty who don't like their bodies; who don't really see themselves as whole. That's so horrible. My body is not perfect, but I love it. It's my perfect, and that's all it ever needs to be.

I want to encourage women to write your own story about life. Be your own author, be your own creator. You were told a story in childhood—you're going to grow up, find your prince charming and he's going to take really good care of you. That's an old story. It doesn't have to be yours. Ask yourself why you are pining for these things, and what is it that you're really missing. If you're honest with yourself—you're going to find out it's you that you're missing. It's not that you're missing having a man in your life. At the core of it is insecurity, and if you deal with that, you're going to be okay. Be your own comfort. Pat your own back. Even if you don't feel like it, stand in the mirror every morning and tell yourself you're one beautiful babe. Why can't you be fabulous? Don't say, *"I can't be,"* instead say, *"Why can't I be?"* Question all that old junk! Don't feed yourself from the troth.

Get yourself a silver platter and have a feast. Stop grabbing for the crumbs that fall to the floor. A big gorgeous spread at the Master's table—that's what you want. And don't settle for anything less!

W<small>HAT GOLDEN NUGGETS DID YOU GET FROM THIS</small>
T<small>REASURE CHEST OF WISDOM</small>?

_____

_____

_____

_____

_____

_____

_____

_____

_____

_____

_____

_____

JOANNE AND BARBARA

Creators of Perri Meno-Pudge,
The Grown-up Cartoon For Women At Midlife
Age: Mid-Fifties

Barbara and I are over fifty and we have basically the same attitude. Midlife is the new beautiful! When we started our cartoon, "PerriMeno-Pudge," we knew we could sit around and complain everyday about what hurts, what doesn't work, and what we can't see. But it was our attitude, that even though we have all these issues, we have so much more that has made all the difference in the world. Everything we've lost because our eyes don't work as well, or our memory isn't quite as good, we get back 100 fold, and in more rewarding ways now.

I need glasses now. I had 20/10 and 20/15 vision until the day I turned fifty, but all that's changed. I see things in my life and in the lives of others around me that I've never seen before, and with clarity I've never known before. I can look at each thing I feel I have lost through my body aging, and see that I've gained so much more internally and spiritually. Barbara and I have found humor to be the best vehicle with which to communicate with other women about the changes that we go through at midlife. Through these silly cartoons, we do little snapshots of frustrations and situations that we've gone up against, that seem to be parallel in every woman's life. We try to bring a sense of community and reassure women their journey is a shared one, because we feel it too. We're breaking the silence and shining a big light on all these issues. This way, when women experience similar emotions in their own lives, they feel less alone.

Our moms didn't talk about hot flashes and menopause; it was a forbidden subject for them. It was almost as though "the change of life" signaled their lives were winding down and ending. Barbara and I feel like it's the beginning of the next part of our life.

"I HAVE TOTAL CONFIDENCE THAT I WOULD NOT TRADE NOW FOR ANYTHING IN THE WORLD. I'M NOT INSECURE ANYMORE. I KNOW WHAT I CAN DO, AND I KNOW HOW GOOD I AM AT WHAT I CAN DO."

I've known Barbara for almost thirty years, and she has always been outspoken, which is one of the things I admire about her. We're in our mid-fifties now, and since she's gotten older she's become even more comfortable in what she says.

Joanne is absolutely right about me; I don't give a hoot about what anybody thinks about what I say. Barbara and I are graphic designers and we worked together for many, many years. We would go out to dinner together with our families on the weekends; our husbands liked each other, our kids nudged each other, and it just worked out very well. We were all out together on one particular evening, and everyone was just annoying the crap out of us, so we just started doodling on a piece of paper. We were telling each other stories back and forth and when the doodle was complete, we called the character, "Pudge."

Barbara happened to have a cat named "Pudge," and the character was originally going to look like a cat. But suddenly we just gasped and screamed "PerriMeno-Pudge!" From there, we developed the characters, pooling the traits of so many women we knew, including our own, but our inside joke is *"any similarities to persons living or deceased, is purely coincidental."* That's our story, and we're sticking to it.

I have total confidence that I would not trade now for anything in the world. I'm not insecure anymore. I know what I can do, and I know how good I am at what I can do. I used to feel like I was pulling the wool over everybody's eyes, or at least trying to. I even have a cartoon someone drew for me, of a little sheep with the wool getting pulled over his eyes. It used to sit on my desk because I always felt I was going to get found out. But the older I got, I realized there was nothing to hide from. I actually did possess the talents I didn't think I had, and I could truly count on myself.

I definitely have to agree with Barbara that I have a completely different attitude about things now. My new fashion sense is, if I can't hide it—I'll decorate it. Just the other day I was thinking about the eyebrows I used to have, that have now changed direction and are growing out of my nose and you know what, I really don't care.

I have a lot of friends, but the ones who are surface friends are clearer to me. It's not that I don't care whether people like me, but if we don't click, that's fine too. I'll just move on and stick with the people who are of a like mind. If you want to get involved in the superficial stuff that happens in life, you're welcome to do that, but I don't have the time for it or the patience for it anymore. I don't care what you look like, I don't care where you come from, I look more at the inner core of a person. Now I find myself really connecting with people who I never thought I would, and I find that I'm more comfortable with who I am.

Yes, I care about the twenty pounds I need to lose, but it's from a health perspective, and not because of reasons of vanity or the need to be thin. I like to look nice and I like to dress well, but I can be 20 or 30 pounds overweight, put something on, and still get compliments from people. They say, *"Wow, you look nice today,"* and I think to myself, *"Yeah, I know!"*

We live in Florida, and in spite of things hurting a little and not being able to move the way we used to, we both enjoy very active lifestyles and do as much as we can; swimming, biking, working out, playing. We both had children a little late in life, Barbara was thirty-seven when she had Gregg, and I was almost forty-one when we adopted our daughter. I have a soon to be high school sophomore who keeps me going. My husband is almost five years younger than I am, so sitting still is not an option.

Never give in to the aging process and let it take over. I try to stay physically active, because if I didn't, it would be over for me.

We all have a choice, we can be whoever we want to be, but we just have to decide who that person is. We can be old at forty, we can be old at fifty and we can be young at sixty. I don't feel any different on the inside, than I did when I was younger. The only noticeable difference is how I can physically approach whatever it is I'm trying to do. We all have obstacles, and we can either use them as excuses, or we can find a way around them. Women are much better at finding a way around them, than men. What we have to do is learn how to reach out to other women. We all have enough talent. Women travel in packs and I think it's for a reason; if you can't do it by yourself, then go find a friend who will help you do it, and likewise, help her with something she needs. Men learn early on how to function as a team, and we don't always do that. But for me, that has attributed to the success in my life. I've been blessed with good, strong girlfriends who don't let me get away with feeling sorry for myself, and won't tolerate hearing me say the words, *"I can't."*

WHAT GOLDEN NUGGETS DID YOU GET FROM THIS TREASURE CHEST OF WISDOM?

_____

_____

_____

_____

_____

CONNIE VASQUEZ

Attorney, Founder of Vintage Awesome

Age 48

I am definitely forty plus and fabulous. I still feel really, really great, I've got all this wisdom and you know what's funny, is that it's not all that serious. By day, I'm a lawyer, but I'm currently in the process of getting out of law and creating "Vintage Awesome;" a blog, lifestyle, travel and event company, designed exclusively for people of a certain age. My aim is to target individuals from 45 – 60, and when I say sixty, I mean like, Dennis Harper sixty, not decrepit and given up on life sixty. If you can complain for hours on end about your knees hurting—you need not apply. You are not vintage awesome. I'm sure you're very lovely, but you're not going to be playing inflatable twister in Central Park.

I'm forty-eight, was born in 1960, had a theater background and then injured my knee. I worked my way through school and became a paralegal. When I went to law school at thirty-seven, it was not your typical age for entering law school. When I entered a firm along with first year associates, I had to deal with the age issue. So I flipped it on its back and said, *"What you are getting from me as a first year associate, instead of someone twenty-four, is thirteen more years of experience in dealing with people."* Clients loved me!

I think what has me in transition is the fact that I'm forty-eight. I do construction litigation, and maybe if I were doing ACLU work, I'd feel differently. But this is not why I'm here, and at forty-eight, I'm not willing to give anymore time over to that. Sure I'm afraid of stepping out, but I have a brilliant coach I've been working with for three weeks. I declared myself ready, and she's been rocking the house with me. I realized in a conversation with her recently, that I could have my concerns and my fears, and listen to all the junk in my head, but then what would I have? Fear and reservation, that's what. If I want something else; something big, luscious, and wonderful, I have got to be willing to come out of that small box. This is a major move for me that I definitely could not have made in my twenties or thirties.

"THE WOMAN I'VE BECOME TODAY IS THE PRODUCT OF MY KEEPING LITTLE BITS OF ME ALONG THE WAY, AND DISCARDING THE PIECES THAT DIDN'T WORK."

Working with a coach has been very beneficial for me. I've coached a lot of Landmark Education programs and it's been an amazing experience and really integral to whom I am today. I've been complaining about my life as a construction litigator for the past three years now, which is just boring. It's wearisome and I refuse to live a boring life. So I imagined myself at a poker table with a bunch of chips, and I made that gesture of "all in" and thought, *"Look, I'm forty-eight and I'm all in."*

The blessing is I have a really good job and, believe me, people think I'm crazy. I might be—who knows? I haven't quit my job yet, and so far I haven't made any horrible mistakes. But I'm really unhappy in my job and feel unfulfilled. So what if I'm making a mistake, it's not like I'm burning up my law degree. What's the worst thing that can happen? I make a terrible mistake and I'm unhappy? I'm already unhappy in this area of my life and it's just not working. What works about it is my paycheck, and I'm blessed and grateful for that. If I can build something on the other side that's mine and that makes me happy—why not? That's the advantage of being a certain age. I have a job and I have a salary, but now I choose to create something for myself, so that I can parachute out of my unfulfilling day job.

I've been divorced since 1992 and have no children. While some may tend to think that makes my decision to leave my job easier, the flipside of it is, I have no second income to fall back on either. I'm not dating, and am back on hiatus from Match.com. I just don't get fifty-something CEO's who behave the way they do. It makes my head hurt.

I love having a man's shirt in my closet, and a drawer filled with my man's stuff, and having him in my house, but I also like my house. I'm not willing to put up with being bored. I'm not willing to put up with rowing the boat alone all the time. I'm not willing to twist myself into a pretzel because I think he's the one and it can work. If I'm twisting into a pretzel, thinking the relationships going to work, guess what? It's not going to, because at some point I'm going to untwist. I may have even turned myself into something he didn't fall in love with. I learned that lesson from a previous relationship.

Waiting for calendar calls at the courthouse, I've heard people sound so boxed in, and they don't see a way to have fun. Sometimes it may be as simple as taking singing lessons or to go kayaking, but you've got to do these things for yourself. You have to have some fun in your life.

The woman I've become today is the product of my keeping little bits of me along the way, and discarding the pieces that didn't work. In my teens and twenties, maybe even in my thirties, I had a chip on my shoulder; was angry, sort of a maverick with a clenched fist. Now I'm more of an *"I Love Lucy"* kind of maverick. I'm funny and I can't help being funny. I'll fall on my face, and sometimes I mess up, and it's still funny. There's no difference between me messing up and you messing up, but the unique thing is that I can laugh at it and it doesn't stop me, and hopefully through that, other people can look at me and see it's not the end of the world.

At our age, women have already gone through that catty and competitive phase. Now I think we're looking out for each other. What we've learned is that there is the *old boy's* network, and we better create the *gals network* and support each other. There are so many groups for women, support for entrepreneurs, support for moms and support in just about every aspect of life. There's so much on our plates, I sometimes wonder if we did the right thing with the women's lib movement. When I see an elderly person or a pregnant woman on the subway, nobody gets up, except the women. A woman will stand up for an old man before a young man will, and that's very interesting. So I think that as we reach a certain age, we realize it just takes too much energy to fight with each other and it doesn't do us any good. It gives us a reputation among men, and in the business world, as being back-biting; it's just a lot of work for such negative results. And there's no fun in it.

My mother said something to me when I turned thirty-five, *"Connie, just remember, gravity is not your friend."* What happens? Do they have a meeting at night and plan a race to the navel? First one to the armpits wins—what? I love the Playtex commercial that's out now. It features normal, everyday looking women, but they're in their bras. There's this one woman who appears to be thirty-something, and she's young, she's happy, whatever. She has her Playtex bra on, and she points towards her shoulders and says, *"They used to be up here, but now they're down here."* That would be me. But hey, I keep my mammograms up, even though the girls are down.

We're in our forties and we are fabulous. Holy cow! Look at what we've seen, look at what we've done and look at what we've overcome. The Civil Rights Act was signed in 1964 by a white president, and today we have a black president. As a lawyer, I worked the polls. I was on the Obama campaign and they sent lawyers out to the polls on Election Day during the primaries to make sure people were not wrongly turned away. There were little old ladies coming out to vote who needed rides, and they never thought they would see this in their lifetime. On primary day, imagine choosing, if you're a democrat, between a woman and a black man. Just look at us now!

WHAT GOLDEN NUGGETS DID YOU GET FROM THIS
TREASURE CHEST OF WISDOM?

LORETTA PETIT

Ordained Elder, Radio Personality, Stellar Award Nominee,
and Personality of the Year

Age 51

We really sometimes make our way on little nuggets everyday. If there is something I can share to encourage someone I may never meet, to want to be their best self—I'm thankful for the opportunity to do that.

My beginnings were so meager, and even sometimes seemed hopeless. I later found out everything that's shiny is not gold, and everything that looks hopeless, is not hopeless. God can take you from the *gutter-most* to the *uttermost*. When I consider what he's done for me, it's not necessarily a rags to riches story. I'm not going to say I'm rich as the world looks at rich but I'm rich in so many other ways. When I look at the attributes, one's character, yes, I am rich in that; in morals and in values and in standards. It has allowed me to look at the world differently and at myself differently. I love me and it wasn't always like that.

I was always a go-getter, self-motivated, and full of dreams and aspirations. I never was a person of resource or knowledge of how to get it done, but I made myself a person of resourcefulness and I learned how to get things done. Pre-forty, I found myself as a single parent divorced, struggling, challenged, beating up on myself, thinking I was a failure, and it slowed me down. When the emotions that one deals with seem to be bigger than life itself, and we're talking about negative emotions at that, it tends to drag you down and that's what happened to me. I was always a person of aspirations but that's where it ended. I would think about it, but never act on anything because I was heavily laden with the challenges and the burdens of life. So pre-forty I was still finding me; the new me, because I had married and now I found myself single once again. I was out there trying to find out who I was and how to feel good about myself again, and how to be the best mother possible in the midst of all I'm dealing with emotionally and mentally, as well as financially.

I'm not the weak link and shy person I used to be. I have found my voice and I use it to make this world a better place. I have learned it is not an emergency every time things don't go my way. I have learned not to give people power over me; not to even hand those keys over. I have learned forgiveness is a big part of my walk; a great part of my journey, because walking in unforgiveness is one of the greatest setbacks. When you don't forgive, you are really giving people control; you're not free to be who you could be because you're so busy being immersed in anger, and the bitterness and hatred will cripple you.

Moving beyond my thirties, I found that I became a calmer person in many respects. I was very much a perfectionist and would drive myself crazy about everything that was not right in my world. I am still a person who has perfectionist tendencies but I'm not as extreme as I used to be, getting irritated and upset about every little thing and everybody. Now I can look at it and say, *"Okay, that needs to be moved,"* and I make myself a mental note and go on. Then, when I'm free to move it—I do. Those tendencies are probably there because I believe in striving for excellence in all things. While we will never reach perfection, it does not mean we should not have pride about what we're involved in, attached to, or what our names go on. Sloppiness is not being your best self. You can have a day when you just let it rest, or have things out of order and let it sit there, but the world was created in order, and I believe we should do things in the same fashion. So my spirit of excellence is different from when I was a pre-forty perfectionist. I am a calmer person now, more focused, and I think my way through things, rather than acting out about things.

I have raised my children and this is time for me now. I'm back in school and have two businesses; one in promotions and public relations that I've run for 10 years, and now and an online store that deals with gift items and products for the home. I recently closed fourteen shows with a musical stage play. Now that my children are grown, I'm taking time for me, doing things I have always wanted to do. I made sure to handle all things concerning them when I needed to be parenting and raising them. However, parenting never goes away. Even though they're grown and most of them are gone, I will always be a mother. But as it relates to carving out time to do the "me" things, I do them.

When we, as women, learn to love ourselves in a healthy way, we won't feel desperate for someone to complete us. I believe women sometimes sell themselves short for a quick thrill, or just to say, *"I have someone."* We don't have to do that. We can still have our standards and values and if he can't agree with what we believe—he's got to move. Let him go and send him packing! We have got to have a healthy self-esteem and know that we are complete. Sure, it's wonderful to have a husband in your life, *if* he's a good husband. But if you don't have that, you can still learn to love life. Find yourself and know who you are. Discover what you like

"WE WANT TO BE AROUND A LONG TIME, BUT WE DON'T WANT TO DISCIPLINE OURSELVES IN ORDER TO TAKE CARE OF OURSELVES. I'M FACED WITH THAT CHALLENGE EVERYDAY. SOMETIMES I'M ASKING THE LORD TO HELP ME TAKE CARE OF ME, AND AT THE SAME TIME, I'M EATING AN OREO COOKIE."

and dislike. Once you find what you're good at, give back to society some of your gifts and talents. If you're financially set, give back some of your resources.

I live by the motto, *"Enjoy life."* What does it take for you to enjoy life? I tell people all the time, if you're on a job and you're not having fun or enjoying it, don't leave the job until you get another one, but start looking for a new one. Only now, look for a job that's going to give you what you need. Yeah, you're there to work, and work is not always fun and games, but in the midst of your work, you should be able to have some joy. If I were an accountant, I would hate the job. I would have to quit immediately because it would drain me. It would make me feel bad every day of my life, and I am not going to put myself in a situation like that. If I'm in a relationship that has me feeling bad every day—that relationship has got to go, whether it's a close girlfriend or a man in my life. You're not going to make me feel bad. Sometimes you've got to cut your circle if everyone around you is unhealthy. I don't care if you've known them since kindergarten. If you find that you've grown in different directions and if they are not contributing something healthy and happy in your life, and are not supportive of the things you do and aspire to be, then you need to set them free. Always have people around you who are going to tell you the truth, and will encourage you in the areas you want to grow in, and who will be there for you in hard times. If those are not the people you have around you, then you need to make some changes.

As long as life lasts we can always work on things. It's a challenge when I look in the mirror and I see my hips and they look like a growth on the side of my body. Remember, that's only a small part of you and you learn to love that too. Tell yourself, *"Okay, you're bigger than I want you to be and I'm going to work on this."* I may not have the power to get the weight down to where I want it to be, but Curves or Jenny Craig could help me. If you don't seem to have the power within yourself, find where the power is. I'm not saying have drastic surgery, but have somebody to coach you to help you work it off and help you to eat healthier. We want to be around a long time, but we don't want to discipline ourselves in order to take care of ourselves. I'm faced with that challenge everyday. Sometimes I'm asking the Lord to help me take care of me, and at the same time, I'm eating an Oreo cookie. So we're going to sink sometimes, but we don't have to sink all the way to the bottom. Start stroking. Start swimming. Get yourself out of that hole and keep working on you. Be the best you that you can be. Be good to people, it doesn't cost anything to share a smile. Love yourself, love your God and enjoy your life.

The Loretta Petit story is still unfolding. Only chapters have been finished, but the book is still being written.

WHAT GOLDEN NUGGETS DID YOU GET FROM THIS TREASURE CHEST OF WISDOM?

_____

_____

_____

_____

_____

_____

_____

_____

_____

CATHERINE HICKLAND

Singer, Actress, State Hypnotist, and Heartbreak Survivor

Age 53

My life began again after 40. And in spite of divorce and other "setbacks," it's even better at 53. Somehow, I always knew it was going to be that way. We get what we expect, and what I've learned for sure is, setbacks are set-ups for comebacks.

I know the meaning of consequence now and I make better choices. I have learned that we can save people from just about anything, except themselves. I morphed my career at 50 and am thrilled with my choice, from television actress to stage hypnotist, author and speaker.

I don't buy into the Madison Avenue ageism, and I had my first book published at 52. I am here to tell you, life and joy begins and ends when we believe it does. My mission is to bust the age myth wide open through my work.

I've been in the entertainment industry since I was seventeen; actress and entertainer in both stage and television. I've always been in a business that is age sensitive, to put it mildly. I have heard about it and I have been victimized by it, and was actually let go from a job because I was forty.

I was working on a show—can't say which one. My boss was a man, a fat slob, exactly my age, but I, who was in the best shape of my life, simply lost my job because, in his eyes, I was too old to be on the show.

"SOMETIMES THE GIFTS WE GET IN LIFE COME IN A PRETTY PACKAGE; BUT SOMETIMES THEY JUST COME WRAPPED IN A HEAVY DOSE OF REALITY."

I had done nothing wrong. I had been there a long time, did my job, saved the company a ton of money, was a totally exemplary employee, so I asked, *"Why am I being let go?"* I was told, flat out, it was my age.

While there was nothing I could do about that, there was something I could do about the way I felt about it. There was something I could do about the way I looked at it. I could have sued them if I really wanted to push it. Or, I could choose to say, *"Thank you so much. I've enjoyed my time here and I'm going to go do something and work somewhere, even if it's just for me, somewhere I am valued and appreciated, and I am going to change this landscape for women everywhere."* It then became my mission to break that glass ceiling of ageism.

So, what did I do? I began dusting off my old dreams. I went back to school and continued to really examine what would make me happy. Then I started doing it. I became a clinical hypnotist. I didn't give up acting, but I've wanted to be a hypnotist since I was a little girl. I had thirty awesome years as an actor and I still act, but it's not that important to me anymore. Hypnosis became very important because I realized doing that was actually going to help the world; changing people's minds, which ultimately changes people's lives.

Shortly after I started doing that, one of my instructors said to me, *"Wow, you should be doing stage hypnosis. You've done broadway, theater, stand up comedy—you're a natural."* So I followed in the footsteps of my girlhood hero, Pat Collins, and started doing stage hypnotism and, lo and behold, what I really find is age doesn't matter—talent does. It takes a lot of talent to do it and people don't care how old you are. As long as you put on an awesome show—you're in. I love that!

I still work as an actress. I became an author and my book, *The 30-day Heartbreak Cure*, was released just a few months ago. It didn't matter how old I was to write it. I'm starting my second book now and I've shifted my priorities and reinvented myself for me. Now I am making a living doing the things I love to do.

Everything begins and ends in the mind. We cannot control the way other people view us, but the truth is, I'm the daughter of the Most High God and He's my agent, manager, best friend and He's in charge. I just show up and do the work. I'm here to tell everybody it's absolutely possible. My life didn't even begin until forty and again, somehow, I always knew it would be that way.

Old is a state of mind. It's negative programming. Being told we're too old is one thing, but believing it and making it so, is another. We must change the mindset of forty being some awful milestone—it's awesome! I got pushed into a new direction and I am so grateful for it. Sometimes the gifts we get in life come in a pretty package; but sometimes they just come wrapped in a heavy dose of reality. The mindset you're in; how you're going to accept, hear, and ultimately, what you are going to do with that information is what makes all the difference.

I didn't realize when I was younger, that I was a little bit more in control of my life than I thought I was. If I had known then what I know now, wow! This is why I am passionate about teaching. When I was in my twenties, I was always kind and considerate. I loved those qualities about myself but, I was also naïve. I didn't understand how people could manipulate us covertly and overtly. I didn't understand there were people who were not like me. I thought that everybody thought the same way I did. As a result, my relationships suffered because I didn't have a model for what a healthy relationship was supposed to be. I was just throwing things out there and seeing what worked. I didn't have a strategy or a plan for my life. I am so grateful that God protected me as much as He did.

Now in my fifties, I realize I am in control of me. I understand the meaning of consequence. Before, I would just act out with the survivor behaviors I gained from growing up in a dysfunctional family which, many people do grow up in. It wasn't until I turned fifty that I started to understand all of it; actions, consequences, being in charge of my life and not caring what other people think. I'm really in the business of me. I have a much better life now than I did in my twenties, thirties or forties.

I've always been very in check with my emotions. That, I think, comes from a childhood where nothing was safe. When a childhood doesn't feel safe to you, you grow up holding a piece of yourself back in relationships. You don't ever hand yourself over so completely to anybody for fear that you'll get crushed. This causes you to do stupid things, resulting in survivor behavior. I was always in check with my emotions, but I didn't think things through. Now, with everything I do, I don't let people talk me into things or rush my decisions. *"No"* is my favorite word. Then there's, *"Let me think about it,"* and after that it's, *"I just told you, I am not ready to make that decision, but I will get back to you when I am able to."* End of story. I have learned that I can say these things and it doesn't make me a bad person. Anyone who is not willing to wait for me to be comfortable with my decision, needs to go away.

I am in month nine of a self-imposed year long sabbatical from dating. When I first started this, I wondered what it would be like; not a single kiss, not a hug, not a date, no handholding or looking into someone's eyes. I thought it would be weird, but it has been anything but that. It has been fantastic. It has deepened every friendship I have and I've even made two new friends. There's no sexual tension or longing. It was a commitment I made to myself with the goal of getting to know myself so completely, inside and out, to realize my goals and dreams and not have to answer to anyone or anything, and to be responsible just to myself. It has been awesome. I'm connecting with people on a much deeper level now. My friendships are incredible, and my male friendships have grown exponentially. People have been so respectful of it and have gotten to know me on a deeper level. I don't know that I'll want to give it up in three months. It's going to be hard. I've really learned to love my own company.

When you make a vow to stand tall in your being, at any age, you become really attractive to people. That includes people who are hiring, people who may want to date you and people who want to be your friend. Choose to use your mind the way God intended it to be used; strong, powerful, knowing your worth, and possessing emotional intelligence. And refuse to accept the illusion someone creates for you—as your reality.

WHAT GOLDEN NUGGETS DID YOU GET FROM THIS TREASURE CHEST OF WISDOM?

_____

_____

_____

_____

_____

_____

_____

_____

_____

ACHARYA SRI KHADI MADAMA

Host of *Yours Truly, Yoga* and recipient of the Jewel of India Award,
New Delhi India, 2009
Age 61

B eing over forty is wonderful. I'm feeling much more confident now and am able to be of service to others. At a younger age, there was always this question of *"Who's going to listen to me?"* Being over forty is like winning a marathon and still remaining in the sport you love.

I live a very interesting life. I've been doing Yoga for over forty years, and started when I was a teenager. I always wanted to perform martial arts, and at forty-eight, I took on the challenge of learning it. I was the only female in the school, and because I had done Yoga for so many years, the fella's in the school, who were all in their twenties, thought I was only thirty. Yoga has kept me very youthful, and my body is still very flexible, pliable and strong.

I first started teaching Yoga in the fall of 1969. People would share amazing testimonies of their results after being in my class for only 10 or 12 weeks. I remember two ladies in particular. One reported that she no longer needed her reading glasses since taking the class, because her vision had improved significantly. The other woman informed me that she no longer required an operation she was supposed to undergo to correct her tilted uterus. When she started my class, she had already scheduled the surgery, and in the interim decided to take up Yoga. When she returned for her pre-op testing, the doctor informed her that she no longer needed the procedure. Her uterus was right where it belonged. I just can't emphasize enough how much Yoga benefits one's overall health and well being.

Martial arts began on top of my Yoga career. At the time, I was on television twice a week promoting *"Yours Truly, Yoga."* I had over 300,000 viewers. Here I was, forty-eight years old and extremely fit for my age, executing forward somersaults and backward rolls. I was performing all the gymnastics the fella's were doing, and I was able to do a lot of routines that they weren't able to do. Thirteen years later, at sixty-one years old, I am still progressing in martial arts and am in three halls of fame. I'm a certified judge now so I get to attend some very high profile martial arts events. The pinnacle of this experience was serving as a judge at the famous "Arnold Schwarzenegger Martial Arts Festival."

"BEFORE I TURNED FORTY, THINGS HIT ME MUCH HARDER THAN THEY DO NOW. I AM BY NO MEANS DESENSITIZED, BUT AM INSTEAD PRIORITIZED."

Every Wednesday I teach my Brazilian Jujitsu fighters. Even today there are things I can do that they cannot. I am the only person I know of who can perform three minute stationary leg lifts, because they are extremely difficult to accomplish.

The thing I am most famous for is using a steel fan and I have won many tournaments and trophies for my performances. I recently presented a workshop at the "World Karate Union," and everyone there thought that I was only forty years old. They absolutely could not believe the positions I was able to get into; low crouching positions, dragon and tiger, all very difficult positions to master. The entire class consisted of young men who were black belts in Karate, and no one could believe I was sixty-one.

Somewhere around my mid-fifties I founded my own system which I call "Fa Shen Training Arts," because I had to find a way to combine my passion for the martial arts and the Yoga that I practiced for so many years. I couldn't throw the baby out with the bath water. Instead, I incorporated all of the Yoga training into my martial arts system, so that it forms the basis for all of the physical culture.

By the time I was in my mid-forties, all of my girlfriends, who are 10-14 years younger than I am, were pretty much hobbling around and complaining about getting older. I couldn't relate to that. I could never relate to the concept that just because you reach a particular number, there are limitations in what you can do. You're expected to develop aches and pains, have difficulty healing and lose muscle strength, all because your body is aging. I'm here to challenge that myth because at sixty-one, I don't even wear reading glasses and I can read even the tiniest print on any package in the grocery store.

Menopause is another challenge that women face in midlife. We are forced to go through menopause due to our reproductive organs, but when you do Chi Kung, you stop the whole process. If you were to start performing Chi Kung, even as early as forty, you will stop your cycle. Your eggs are still there, but you will no longer get your period. It's not unhealthy. It's a known fact that the longer you have your period, the greater your odds are of developing uterine cancer.

You have to reinvent yourself. As a professional Yoga therapist and instructor of forty years, as well as a TV celebrity, if I didn't reinvent the wheel, and in my case it was the Yoga wheel, I would be in trouble. If I were still trying to function in my classes today, the way I did back in the 1970's, I wouldn't be able to compete and keep up with everyone. When I was a yoga instructor in New Jersey, back in 1969, I was only one out of seven that existed at the time. Now there are thousands. If a woman doesn't have a challenge, she becomes bloated, feels empty and unfulfilled inside. No other human being is capable of fulfilling you or making you happy. It's your personal responsibility to have a quest in life and create it for yourself.

I do things that bring me joy, whether it's folding laundry or canning tomatoes during the summer. I constantly challenge myself and I'm certainly not sitting around waiting for the Grim Reaper to arrive. You're either going to get old, sick, or die, if you don't move ahead in life.

The older you get, the more mature you become. You are able to gain the experience you need to continue to formulate a better version of yourself. At sixty-one, I am now more emotionally flexible and stronger than I was at forty. Before I turned forty, things hit me much harder than they do now. I am by no means desensitized, but am instead, prioritized. After forty, you get to a point where you've been around long enough to know that somehow, things are going to work out.

I see a lot of women out there who are just as emotionally immature as they were at nineteen because they're not working on themselves. A lot of people don't know this about me because when they see me, I'm always smiling and positive, but I have suffered through some very serious and deep depressions for most of my life. I was not on medication, because I felt I should have enough wisdom and knowledge to be able to heal myself. As a consequence, I battled this dark cloud alone for most of my life.

Somewhere in my forties a shift began to take place because I continually worked on myself. I was determined to overcome this depression and stared the dark cloud hovering over me right in its face, and forced myself to begin the healing process.

When I train my fighters I tell them, *"You really only have one opponent, and it's you. It doesn't matter who the other face is in the ring, you're really only battling yourself."* Your first enemy is inside of you. At sixty one, I had earned six black belts and was inducted three times into the hall of fame. None of that would be possible if I had chosen to say home, watch TV and eat bon-bons all night. You have to stay on top of your game.

If you talk to young people, you'll notice that they are always planning ahead, trying to accomplish something that they've always wanted to do. Sometimes older people reflect back on how it used to be and no longer have a quest in life. You have to create exciting plans for yourself in order to keep life interesting.

I'm saddened by women in their forties and fifties who were once very vital, and now can barely get up and down a flight of stairs due to their poor physical health. For a fifty-something grandmother, not to be able to get down on the floor and play with her grands, and get back up again because of her weight or the strain on her joints, breaks my heart. Please take whatever steps are necessary to preserve your body and remain strong and flexible, in order to be able to move around freely and without effort.

Do whatever you have to do to fully participate in life. Mae West said it best, "You're never too old to become younger."

WHAT GOLDEN NUGGETS DID YOU GET FROM THIS TREASURE CHEST OF WISDOM?

TINA STULL

NHRA Drag Racer
Age 44

I can honestly say my life as a strong woman did not begin until my late thirties. It was the backdrop for entering my forties, which I think is a time when a woman has the greatest amount of time and ability to accomplish her dreams or any other plans she may have. When you're twenty—you think you know everything, and may have dreams, but no tools to realize them. When you're thirty—you're usually struggling in a learning curve. Now that you're forty, you have the resources to make the dreams come true. I've been able to do things that when I was in my twenties I never thought were possible. Forty definitely marks the beginning of the second half and best part of your life.

So often, we want perfection in a certain area, regardless of whether we've trained properly or not. I find myself getting frustrated trying to create crafts, because I want my crafts to look as good as the lady who's been doing it for twenty years. We expect perfection from ourselves without training. When I decided to pursue racing, my then husband was a Green Beret, and he used to say, *"You're born knowing nothing. If it can be taught, you can learn it."* And it's true. The only reason you can't do something is because no one has taught you.

When I made up my mind to race, I realized I had to learn, and the only way to learn is through making mistakes. Nobody has to tell you not to touch a hot iron. At some point in our lives we've been burned by one and the lesson is imprinted in our brains forever. I looked at the list of things that could go wrong in racing, and gave myself permission to make those mistakes. At the same time, there is no way someone can warn you of every possible thing that could go wrong. *"Don't catch the parachute lever on your pants when you try to get into the car, or you're going to deploy it! Don't forget when you plug in your battery charger, to make sure the cord isn't plugged in to something else."* They may sound like stupid little rules, and when you first hear them you're thinking, *"Oh, I'd never do that,"* and then you go and do it.

"WHEN I REALIZED I DIDN'T HAVE FOREVER, THE VALUE OF MY TIME SOARED THROUGH THE ROOF."

I was driving down the track once, and my front wheel suddenly started to wobble like mad. I pulled off the gas pedal and tried to stop it as quickly as possible. I got out of the car to check and see what was wrong, and noticed that three of the four bolts that held my front wheel were missing. Who would have thought to check? If somebody told you everything that could go wrong, I can assure you, that you'd never get in the car again.

In 2002, I was diagnosed with stage three terminal cancer; cutaneous T-cell lymphoma, which is an extremely rare cancer that causes the T-cells to attack the skin. I hit the internet and learned that the survival rate was only 3-5 years. I was very ill, had no energy and didn't feel well. At the time, I had been holding on to the dream of racing for three years. The car now just sat in my driveway. I'd start it up, and that was it. I had never even gotten to the track. When I received the diagnosis of terminal cancer, I squashed the *notion of racing the following year.* I took a good look at my life. I had an 8 year old daughter, a quadriplegic husband, served on the volunteer fire department, the PTA and the board of directors. I thought, *"If I have 3 years of good life left, or even one year, where am I going to apply it?"*

I realized then that I wanted to have a legacy to leave behind. I had a short amount of time left, to squeeze in a lifetime worth of being a mother. I came to the realization that I was not getting any fulfillment from all the things I was involved in, and I didn't understand why. I finally decided I did not want to do all of those things anymore and was determined not to feel guilty about my decision. I wasn't going to put up with the "BS" from the fire department or from anyone else. I was going to do what I wanted to do, for whatever time I had remaining.

I now felt this sense of urgency about me. Then—I went in for a check up—and they couldn't find the cancer! The doctors at MD Anderson Cancer Center originally told me that there was no way I could be healed, and that this type of cancer did not go into remission. The nine pathologists who reviewed the biopsy, and performed the die marker and genetic tests, all agreed I had the cancer, and now it was completely gone. It was nothing short of a miracle, and I was elated to have my life back.

When you have a quadriplegic husband they always come first. Partially because of the helpless condition they're in and the consequences of not meeting their needs can be drastic. If they're tired and want to get out of a chair, you have to assist them because they are unable to perform any task alone.

Quadriplegics are used to getting their own way because people feel guilty and pity them. They get conditioned to always having things their way and become spoiled. The more they get, the more they want, and eventually even that's not enough. My husband took his frustrations of living in a chair out on me. I don't think it was intentional. It's just such a heavy burden to live life in a wheelchair, lose your independence and be totally cared for by someone else. I had this responsibility for four years following his return home from the military, in 1998. When I was diagnosed with cancer, he left. He emotionally pulled away and just quit.

I do not feel self pity. I don't discount what he had to go through on a daily basis because the burden he carried was significant. Losing his arms and legs and then, God forbid, his wife and caregiver, and knowing he'd have to take care of his step-daughter alone, was a huge responsibility. One I feel became too much for him to handle. Perhaps too, he felt partially responsible for the fact that I was so worn down. It took a lot out of me to care for him. Despite that, we still managed to do things together. We'd go to the beach, go swimming, travel across the country, tried scuba diving and even snow skiing. You have to become really creative to do some of these things but we didn't let the chair stop us. The reality of having lost his arms and legs and now possibly losing his wife scared him, so he left rather than face these challenges. We've never spoken about it. In fact, we've never really spoken again since he left.

Believe it or not, his departure was a huge gift to me. For the first time in my life I could say, *"I don't want to."* We go through life with so much stuff stuck to us, like static socks. We don't feel comfortable saying, *"Hey, get off me"* because it doesn't seem nice. When I realized I didn't have forever the value of my time soared through the roof. If I'm dying in three years what financial risks am I willing to take now? You begin to think about things with a whole new perspective. The whole experience of cancer was the greatest gift I've ever received, and as horrible as it was, I wouldn't wish it on my worst enemy. There are parts of this experience that changed me to the core. It hurts, but it gave me a completely new and open outlook towards my future.

If you try to ignore the fear, it doesn't go away. My favorite saying has always been *"Feel the fear and do it anyway."* If you think you can't move forward until you're not afraid, you won't go anywhere. But if you face the fear, evaluate it and ask, *"What's the worst thing that can happen?"* the answer won't kill you and you'll move through it. I've been to a point in racing where I've been so frightened, that I've actually broken out in hives and had to see a doctor for a shot. Although I knew the car was safe the fear wasn't going to go away until I conquered it. I knew I had the skill and ability to do it, so I forced myself. What was the worst thing that could happen? For me, it wasn't crashing the car. It was going out there, looking like an idiot in front of this brand new group of guys I barely knew, and have them think badly of me. More people are held back by that, and that is what I consider being a true failure.

Standing up for myself in the racing arena was difficult at first. The drivers there were really well versed and knew a lot more than I did. There were times when they knew I was right, but they also knew that I didn't know how to defend my argument. I had to go in there and prove myself, time and time again. If I say something is wrong with the car—then something is wrong with the car! I finally got to the point where I had earned enough respect, and people started listening to me and stopped challenging me.

I've cut some people out of my life. Mainly, the ones who come to you every eight months with the same problems. Even though you continue to advise them it's always the same thing, over and over again. They refuse to listen and always come with the same issues. I look at my life and when I see the same issues arise, I get mad at myself—not at the problem. What am I not learning that causes this problem to reoccur? Once I'm honest with myself, I know that a big part of it is going to become my responsibility.

We live mediocre lives because we have free will. There are times in my life I took the easy way out. I dodged the opportunity for growth and maturity. I avoided responsibilities because they were either uncomfortable or I thought they weren't fun. That's what you do when you're young. At some point you realize that you want to grow and reach your full potential. If you want to be bigger than your own ability, you'll stop sitting around waiting to cash in your lottery ticket and do something that will take you out of your comfort zone.

For the first time in my life I have confidence in who I am, and realize that I don't need permission from a spouse, parent, or friend, to do what I want with life. I now know my path well enough to be confident in whatever it is I'm doing, even if other people disagree.

Bad things happen to all of us, but these experiences should not diminish us as women. You better be a better you at forty-one than you were at forty. You better be a better you at fifty than you were at forty-nine. If you haven't improved in some area of your life, then you haven't been doing your job at living. Our job is to just keep growing and become a better person. I still have areas where I want to improve. I want to be more patient, kinder, and have better discernment. I want to be able to stand my ground and yet still be fair to others. I want to be less emotional, and more business minded, and to have greater compassion and the wisdom to know when to use it. I want to constantly improve myself.

A friend of mine used to say, *"Your past ended at midnight. Today is a new day."* You get a clean slate every day and a chance to start over. It's what you do from here on in that truly matters. As a gift to myself, I'm keeping the good, and I'm letting the rest go.

WHAT GOLDEN NUGGETS DID YOU GET FROM THIS TREASURE CHEST OF WISDOM?

_____

_____

_____

_____

_____

_____

_____

_____

JUDIE BUCHOLZ

Regional Dean – Onsite Programs, Strayer University
Age 51

My career was pushed further after I turned forty. I was not as driven before then. It wasn't until after forty that I was motivated to go to the next level. It was then I decided I wanted more out of life than just aging. Now I'm doing what I want to do, and I absolutely love my job. I work for fantastic people, and I'm making a difference in others lives, more so than I would have if I had stayed in a typical classroom. Not only do I make a difference for the instructors, but I also make a difference for the students.

When I was in the military, I was just working and performing a job. Not that I didn't love my job, because I really did. It was a difficult time for me. It felt like I didn't have a career, that it was just a job. After I turned forty, I was more interested in establishing a career. I thought about what I wanted to do with the rest of my life that was going to make a difference.

I retired for the first time at the age of thirty-nine. It was nice, but it was not what I wanted to do with the rest of my life. There was no purpose in it. Now I feel a deep purpose in what I do, and I'm more in control of my destiny. I have more choices and have more options. Whether they're good for me or not, I'm not afraid to make these decisions. I now do what I'm most comfortable with. I didn't do that before I turned forty, I only did as I was told. Now I have more say in what I do.

It's very common today to see fifty and sixty year olds in school. I think it's a great thing because they're achieving their personal goals. They're establishing support groups with other women, mentoring and helping each other to take that first step. It's just taking the first step that can be difficult. We can do whatever we want to, but we just need to have the courage, guidance and encouragement to do it.

"THE WORLD IS MY PLAYGROUND, BECAUSE I CHOOSE IT TO BE. I AM NOT GOING TO STOP GROWING AND DEVELOPING BECAUSE I'M OVER FIFTY. I REFUSE TO COMMIT TO A MIDLIFE CRISIS."

I entered the military at nineteen years old and served for twenty years. In military terms, I'm considered 70% disabled, based on how different I was from the time I joined the military, until the time I left. It was for various reasons; my knees, my hips, and because I had to have a hysterectomy. They labeled me as being depressed because my husband died while I was in the service, and they said that I suffered from post traumatic stress disorder.

Service connected disability does not equate to civilian sector disability, so I don't receive social security. I'm not falling apart or anything, but I do have some limitations. I'm never going to run again, but it's not good for women anyway, so who cares? I can't have anymore kids, but I have a beautiful daughter who is about to give birth to a baby, so that doesn't bother me at all.

Depressed? Yes I was. My husband had been murdered, so what did they expect, that I would have a party? Those labels don't define me and they never have. The labels made it convenient for the military to manage me. I know me, and I know what my capabilities are, so they can't manage me anyway. You have to understand that people develop a sense of comfort when they label someone. They don't know what to do with you when you don't conform to their expectations. I set my own expectations for my life.

I always promised my husband that I would go back to school, get my PhD, and let him retire. When he died, I felt obligated to finish earning my degree. Part of my dissertation was based on misunderstood grievers. Not all grief is the same. People tend to misunderstand the grief of murder or homicide survivors. If your child dies, you experience a different type of grief. Sudden loss, as opposed to losing someone who has Alzheimer's disease, or someone who has cancer, is totally different. A publishing company read the abstract from my dissertation, and asked me to turn it into a book, and I did.

After attaining my PhD, I went on to earn another master's degree in technology. I like to learn, and you can never know too much. I'm currently in school again, working on another MBA. Midlife is the greatest time for a woman to be back in school, because you have more self-confidence. You have so many more opportunities to break into various fields. Although the material may be repetitive, and it may involve things you've already seen before, you can still learn so much from interacting with other students. The diversity in the classroom, the discussions, along with the different generations in the workplace and life experience, all provide valuable lessons. They can help you avoid certain pitfalls, or perhaps spark interest in other areas to explore and move your life in another direction.

I'm more confident now, and more secure, and I'm far from finished with improving myself. The world is my playground because I choose it to be. I am not going to stop growing and developing because I'm over fifty. I refuse to commit to a midlife crisis. That's a mind game we play with ourselves. We have self induced doubts about our skills and abilities, and many people choose to go through a midlife crisis when, in fact, we don't really need to. If you have confidence in yourself and believe in what you're doing—you can do anything.

My travel schedule leaves me little time for dating, and I actually prefer it that way. It's only because I am more successful when I am on my own, and not caught up in the guilt trip of spending time with someone, not doing this or that, or worrying about someone else's career coming before mine. I miss companionship, but I work so much that I don't have time to even think about it. Men are nice, I love 'em, but I don't need 'em. I don't ever want to be in a position where I become so dependent on someone. That's not to say I won't get married again, because someday I will. However, I want a man who can help me get to where I want to go and not try to stop me.

I've been married a couple of times, where the man had a problem when I became more successful than him, perhaps because I was so ambitious and wanted to go further than he did. I refuse to be with someone who's going to slow me down. I'm not going to depend on someone else to make me happy.

Most people tell me that I don't look fifty. I certainly don't act fifty, or at least not the fifty that it used to be. Unfortunately, I don't exercise or eat like I'm supposed to, but I'm okay with who I am. If someone can't accept me for the way I look, that's their problem, not mine. I dress and act professionally, and as far as I'm concerned, that's all I need to do. Since I spent twenty years in the military, I'm very conscious about my weight, so I make adjustments when I need to. I don't intend to have plastic surgery, and I'm not going to kill myself attempting to go to the gym or run, which I know I will never do. I'm comfortable with who I am. If we all look the same, life's going to become pretty boring.

I could say I have regrets in life, but, I don't. I'm very happy with life. Yes, I've gone through some bad times, and I've learned from my experiences. If I could do it over, I would probably make some different choices, but I don't regret anything that I've been through. Life is good. My most important life lesson has been not to depend on anyone else to take care of you; learn to do it yourself.

Being a lifelong learner is essential. You always need to keep your skills marketable, and you always need to develop and grow in new ways, because you never know what's going to happen in life. If a perfect job were to come along tomorrow, do you have what it takes to get where you want to go? Keep your skills honed. If a job is offering free training, you need to take advantage of that opportunity. It doesn't matter if it's

"Woodworking 101," you never know where it may lead. There may even be a new hobby in it for you. Keep up with technology. If not, you'll fall behind and become lost, leaving the twenty year olds the opportunity to take over and run the world.

As older women, we have a moral obligation for setting an example to the younger women. We are changing the way women are viewed, and the way they are appreciated and valued. The older a woman becomes, the more valuable she is, because she has acquired the wisdom and confidence she needs, after years of multitasking as a student, teacher, wife, cook, mother, money manager, homework checker, and corporate survivor, all rolled into one. You can't touch her. She's forty plus and fabulous!

WHAT GOLDEN NUGGETS DID YOU GET FROM THIS TREASURE CHEST OF WISDOM?

YOLANDA CARR

Doctoral Student and Grants Coordinator, University of Arkansas

Age 46

I have grown up to be a strong woman of color and have accomplished more in my life than I ever expected. There are still some things I reflect back on and could have done differently, but for the most part, I am proud of the many obstacles I overcame.

I went through a lot of tough times as a child, and it is a blessing that I survived it all.

My daddy was unfaithful in his marriage, and he had affairs left and right. I was forced to leave Louisiana, to get away from it all, because it was so humiliating to hear people in the stores talking about my mother, and remarking on how stupid she was. On Friday's, my daddy would come home from work, pack a bag, walk out the door dressed up and smelling good, and turn to us and say, *"I'll see you later."* We wouldn't see daddy again until Sunday evening. My dad wasn't a bad man, but he was a womanizer. I moved away because I needed to see what else was out there and knew there had to be more the world could offer, than the current situation I was in. I had to run away from the humiliation, even though my mother stayed and was determined to deal with it. I remember her telling me once, that my dad would get his just rewards, and that I shouldn't act resentfully towards him. That was the final straw for me, and it was at that moment when I decided I needed to move on.

It took some time, but over the years I've had a chance to think and put some things into perspective. After many years, I'm finally able to erase all the pain and anger I had towards my dad because of what he had done to my mother. Now when I see him, I can actually show him true love, but it took a very long time for that to happen.

In my twenties and thirties, I thought I was fully grown. The truth is, I was still wet behind the ears and had not matured. Now that I'm in my forties, I'm able to make good, concrete, stable decisions that I know I won't regret. It wasn't that way when I was in my twenties. Now I'm more solid and on task with what it is I want to accomplish.

"I AM SO THANKFUL FOR THE NEW MINDSET THAT I HAVE NOW, AND THAT I WAS ABLE TO SHED THE OLD AND LIMITING BELIEFS THAT CAME FROM MY IMMATURITY AND LACK OF CONFIDENCE."

When you feel like you're in your darkest hour, you have to remember that there is a higher source there for all of us. When you think one door has closed in your face, you have to remember that another one will open. I'm a witness to that. I married in my mid-thirties, and my darkest hour came after my divorce, when I was having some major financial issues. During my marriage, I was the one with the good credit. Although my husband didn't have bad credit, he didn't have any credit at all, which made him a risk in the eyes of lenders. Consequently, all of the credit and bills had to be placed in my name. During the marriage, we never had any financial problems. He always paid the bills on time. Things changed once we split up, and he decided he was no longer going to pay for anything. Everything was in my name, and I was stuck holding this huge mound of debt.

Over a period of time, the weight of it became unbearable. Creditors called constantly, and it seemed that the more I paid, the more they wanted from me. I was so ashamed, that I never reached out to anyone to ask for help. If I had done that, someone may have been able to give me guidance and direction, but I was just too embarrassed to let anyone know. One day, while I was sitting in my apartment, I became very upset. I lived on the third floor, and walked out onto the balcony. I sat there completely overwhelmed and in tears. I can remember looking at the railing and thinking to myself, *"If you jump over this railing, you would probably kill yourself, and you would no longer have to worry about all the bills and the pain you're going through, trying to pay all of these creditors who are constantly calling you, telling you how awful you are, because of your debt."* But then, I heard another voice say to me, *"Yolanda, you know if you jump off that balcony, you're going to hell. If you jump, you're going straight to hell, and you will not see my face."* So I guess you know what I did. I went back inside, got out a pen and pad, made a list of all the debt, and created an action plan. I realized that there were people out there in worse situations than I was in, and this was not worth ending my life. I had to go without a lot of things, and although I didn't want to, I had to get some help from my parents. But I did what was needed, and I finally was able to dig myself out of that hole.

That situation taught me a lot. We are never alone, and there are people out there who can help us, but we have to be able to express our needs. There is nothing we go through in life that someone else has not experienced. Seek help from someone you can trust, because there's always a solution to solve your problems. I will never find myself on a balcony again, thinking about ending my life. What a waste that would have been.

I am in the prime of my life right now, feeling great and am truly blessed. Fortunately, I am healthy, energetic and without any medical problems. I'm currently employed as a Grants Coordinator at the University of Arkansas, in Fort Smith, and taking on this job was a bold move for me. After living in Greensboro, N.C. for almost nineteen years, I decided it was time for a change. Moving here has really given me plenty of time to sit back and reflect on things I wanted to do at this point in my life. This has been a really positive move for me.

One thing I've always wanted to do is earn my doctorate degree. With some persuasion and encouragement from friends at the university where I am employed, I decided to apply for a Doctorate in Workforce Education, with a concentration in College Administration. This is very exciting, and it's something I've always wanted to do. When I obtained my master's degree in 1999, I promised myself I would pursue this. Ten years later, an opportunity has presented itself, allowing me to obtain this degree. I applied and was accepted into the program and I'm definitely going to achieve my goal.

When we were young, forty-five seemed old. Today, it's not. I don't feel or look forty-five, in the stereotypical sense. I wake up every day vibrant and full of life, and I possess an inner peace. When I get dressed in the morning, I know that I look good and don't need anyone to confirm that. I receive compliments throughout the day, but even if I didn't, I still know that I look good. I am very conscious about eating better, taking care of myself, and surrounding myself with positive individuals. I feel renewed, especially with the move, the job and now, working on my doctorate.

I am so thankful for the new mindset that I have now, and that I was able to shed the old and limiting beliefs that came from my immaturity and lack of confidence. I used to feel that if a woman did not have a mate, people would look down on her as though something was wrong with her. Either she had difficulty getting along with someone, or she just wasn't successful when it came to relationships. Those beliefs created a lot of unnecessary stress for me, especially after my marriage failed. When I married, I expected like so many other women did, that it would last forever. When it ended I was so embarrassed, and did not want to tell anyone that we had separated. I just got completely caught up in the perception and worry about what other people would think. I'm now free from that type of thinking.

Women over forty are smart, because we had to overcome many obstacles in life, and we're now better educated and more well-rounded people. We are now strong enough to take on nontraditional jobs in our careers, and participate in politics, standing up for the rights of ourselves and for others. We're more vocal and more visible.

I love the way I look now, much more than when I was younger. We have to be realistic, and know that the older we get, the more our bodies will change. It's up to us to decide just how we are going to deal with those changes, both physically and mentally. It bothered me a little when I first noticed the grey hairs and the extra fat around my stomach, hips and thighs. You just have to have the courage to change the things you can.

I started exercising, walking more, and am selective about what I eat. If you start doing what is within your power—you will notice a difference. It's all about our attitudes and how we choose to take care of ourselves.

My trademark is my smile, and you will never catch me without one. People comment on it all the time. When people see me smiling, it appears that I'm always happy, even though there are times when I feel differently inside. I believe in remaining positive about all situations. I live by the motto, *"This too, shall pass,"* and it always does. Right now, I am so grateful to be alive, to have great friends, and to be able to wake up and go to work every day and be around people I love.

A lot can happen that can ruin a woman's life such as child abuse, sexual abuse, and domestic abuse. These experiences can haunt and rob a woman of being her best self and I was determined not to let that happen to me. My daddy was not physically abusive, but he was verbally abusive. Forgiveness saved my life. When you don't forgive, you give away your power.

Forgiveness and making a conscious decision to let go of the pain and the hurt, allows you to be happier and have more successful relationships. You are free now to move forward and do the things in your life that you've always wanted to do.

My future is bright because I'm still coming up with new and exciting things to accomplish. After I earn this doctorate, I want to become Vice President of a university, so I can be in charge, and just tell everyone else what to do!

WHAT GOLDEN NUGGETS DID YOU GET FROM THIS
TREASURE CHEST OF WISDOM?

ANDREA VANESSA WRIGHT

Associate Executive Director, Hayes Taylor YMCA
Co-founder Warriors, Inc.
Age 50

This is really empowering!

Life is a journey. Life is not always good, and it's not always bad. I have such an excitement for the life I have experienced, thus far. The high school experience, going to college, getting married, and raising my children, are all things that I can now look back on and say *"Been there, done that!"*

I've recently celebrated my 50th birthday, and yes, this is my time now. A lot of women this age are celebrating being here and establishing the ground rules for moving forward. Those rules are not necessarily all about them, because at this stage of the game, we really have a heart for reaching back and helping others.

I personally feel there's never been a better time in my life than now. I've accomplished many of the things I have set out to do, both in my career and personal life. In my financial life, there is still room to grow, and I still have time to get it right. Had I started earlier working on securing my financial future, I'd pretty much be set right now. I deserve to take a cruise or a vacation of my choice every year. The only missing piece of the puzzle is the financial one. But the beauty of it is, I get to take what I know now, and work to improve that area of my life.

The best way to describe me in my youth would be naive and dumb. I was very trusting and impulsive, which often times placed me in precarious situations. I've had my share of hard knocks, but they made me the woman I am today. There is a wisdom now that prevents me from doing things the way I used to.

I have a different approach to life now, and understand that everything I do has a purpose to it and a lesson to learn. Everything now connects to my purpose in life, unlike when I was in my twenties and thirties and was totally clueless. Now, every move I make is about empowering others. I have to make sure that everything I do is for the good of the total community, not just for my family and friends.

I've always had a passion for children and families. I've now gone from the programmatic side, to more of the management and administrative side. I really enjoyed the program side of it, because it was so much more hands on. Due to my present limited physical abilities, I can no longer do many of the things I enjoyed doing with the Girl Scouts, such as camping, and teaching outdoor and survival skills.

You have to be very flexible in this life if you're going to survive it successfully. When you're on a particular path, be the best you can be, using all the knowledge and skills available to you. Understand that the path you're on is subject to change at any moment. Be mindful that at times, we make the wrong choices. Sometimes we hear the voice directing us toward one path, and we choose to take the opposite one instead. If the road you chose leads you into a valley, start climbing back up again.

Several years ago, I experienced a tragic event that would change my life forever. About four weeks prior to this occurring, I was sitting down talking with a group of friends about the hustle and bustle in life and our need to slow down. One friend commented, *"You're going to slow down, but it's going to take something tragic for you to do it."* Within five weeks...boom! I was in a car accident that brought my life to a complete standstill.

I remember rounding a curve heading home from work, just before getting hit. I recall people being present at the scene of the accident and my husband and mother walking up to me, giving me the thumbs up signal in an attempt to reassure me that I was okay. It was about that time a fireman climbed into the car with me, and told me that my legs were crossed. I remember being confused by that, because I felt as though I was sitting normally behind the steering wheel. The last thing I remember was being cut out of the car. After that, I don't recall anything more, until I woke up in the hospital about a week later.

"I NEVER ALLOWED MYSELF TO HAVE A PITY PARTY. IN FACT, I'VE TRIED TO HAVE ONE— IT JUST WON'T HAPPEN. ALTHOUGH I WAS BROKEN UP FROM THE FLOOR UP, ALL I COULD SAY WAS, 'THANK YOU, JESUS!'"

The doctors then informed me about the severity of my injuries. From my hips down, and on both sides of my body, I had a number of severed bones, ligaments, toes, ankles, and muscles. I thought to myself, *"It's okay, I'm going to be alright."* There was difficulty with my legs healing and concern about losing my right leg. The doctors were determined to try everything they could to save it. I would undergo eleven surgeries before having to make the decision to amputate the leg. All I could think of was, *"I can buy another leg, so let's go ahead and just do it!"* While undergoing all these surgeries, the doctors, nurses and staff at Baptist Hospital were absolutely wonderful, but now I was ready to get back to living life. Choosing not to have my leg amputated was life threatening, so I didn't have any other option. Throughout this challenging and painful ordeal, I experienced only one real meltdown. After that, my sole focus was to get better.

In the blink of an eye, I went from being totally self-sufficient and living an active life, to one of complete helplessness. I could barely do anything for myself, and it gave me time to think. I began to really reflect on where I was in life. Up until that point, my life had been one of work, work, and work. I was always trying to do and be everything for everyone else, whether at work, church, or home. The accident gave me an opportunity to do exactly what I needed to do, which was to remain still and reflect. I thought about my work, marriage, family and my relationships with other people in the community, and everything else in between.

I know I inconvenienced some folks, and it placed a huge burden on my husband and two sons. But they held it together for the most part. The toughest test was coming home and having to totally depend on them, and that's when we all experienced breakdowns. My husband was challenged to the max; with having to take care of me, plus do the housework, and satisfy the boy's needs. My youngest son was not driving at the time, and all of the things I did for them as their mother, now became my husband's sole responsibility. Men oftentimes just cannot handle this type of pressure, and I knew this situation was going to test our marriage. It quickly became apparent that there were some serious issues in our relationship that had not been resolved.

People tell me all the time that they're just blown away by the strength and determination I showed in this dire situation, but I had no other choice. There were simply no other options for me, than to play the hand I was dealt. A lot of fortitude came from my strong faith in God. As the songwriter says, *"If it had not been for the Lord on my side..."* I was thoroughly grounded spiritually, and never for a moment doubted that I could overcome everything that happened.

I never allowed myself to have a pity party. In fact, I've tried to have one—it just won't happen. Although I was broken up from the floor up, all I could say was, *"Thank you, Jesus!"* I was grateful for the opportunity to expose and reveal exactly what I needed to be doing with my life.

Before the accident, my business partner and I founded a non-profit organization called Warriors, Inc. Due to our hectic lives, we never found the time to devote ourselves totally and get it up and running. My recovery period now afforded me plenty of time to focus on the organization, write the by-laws, and get the foundational pieces of the company in place.

Today, Warriors, Inc. is alive and well. It's all about empowerment for women 18-40 years old. We believe that in order to empower the community, we have to empower the women first.

In October, we have an honors banquet scheduled. The banquet is being held in recognition of four women who have come through our program and have made some major accomplishments. The symbolic piece is that we will be passing the baton to them, because it's now their turn to help the group of women coming up behind them. When we host the honors banquet next year, this year's honorees will pass the baton on to the women who they assisted through the program. It's all about empowerment, and we hope to keep passing the baton and paying it forward.

Know who you are, and where you are going in life, because life will continue to move forward, with or without you. Surround yourself with positive people. In our youth, we tend to surround ourselves with anybody who calls us their friend, but as we mature, we cut the list.

We long to be around people who understand the journey. So, understand the journey and just enjoy the ride.

WHAT GOLDEN NUGGETS DID YOU GET FROM THIS TREASURE CHEST OF WISDOM?

_____

_____

_____

_____

_____

MINNIE FORTE-BROWN

Professor, North Carolina Central University
Chairwoman, Durham Public Schools Board of Education
Appointee, North Carolina Council of Women
Age 60

*F*orty Plus and Fabulous is a mindset* that we, as women, have to grasp knowing that as we age, we still are every bit as beautiful, and now even more gorgeous than ever before. We have to convey this way of thinking to all women, so they feel and understand if you're no longer twenty years old, life isn't over. Forty is the fabulous new thirty, and when you turn fifty, it will be the new forty. I'm sixty, and not trying to look twenty, because I'm fabulous right where I am now.

I feel that baby boomers, or children of baby boomers, realize that life is for the living and is to be enjoyed. It's important to take care of this temple that God has given you by honoring it and only allowing things inside that are healthy for you. As the aging process begins, there are certain things that naturally occur, and you need to take them in stride and keep moving.

This is the best time of life for me because I am more in control. Clearly, God is in control of everything, but He has allowed me to have some free will, and with that I am able to chart my own course. That's what makes growing older better. My child is now grown, and my grandchildren are well past the toddler stage, and I am just happy with where I am. I'm on my third marriage now, and feel blessed to have had three husbands.

I love life and waking up every morning thankful, not only to see another day, but for the opportunity to make a difference in somebody's life. I'm an educator, so every day I interact with no less than 75-100 young people, and feel compelled to impart something meaningful into their lives. Since I'm a communications professor, it's all about life, and I want them to realize that this journey is one that needs to be enjoyed. You're going to have valleys, and you're going to have mountaintop experiences, and you have to take them both in stride and learn from them. You should welcome everything that happens in your life, because somehow it's preparing you for another step.

Being with these young people everyday is another thing that keeps me feeling young. They haven't given up on life and aren't angry about life, and they add energy, excitement and innovation to this journey.

At twenty, I was wild and crazy while in college. I was experimenting with life and trying to decide what I wanted to do; become an actress or a teacher. Then I became pregnant and had a baby without a husband, and tried to navigate how to raise this beautiful little girl all alone. I asked God to give me the strength to do what I needed to do.

I had a mother who was so strong, open, and so wonderful, that my getting pregnant without being married was never an issue for her. She made it clear that I was to do what I had to in order to take care of this baby and finish college. She was always empowering and accepting and loving, and I'm thankful to have been blessed with a mom like that. I spent everyday finding out something new about myself, and accepted and liked who I was.

I didn't marry until I was thirty, and I gave the marriage a two year time limit. If by then I realized it wasn't what I wanted it to be, I would leave. Within two years, I knew he was not the person I wanted to spend the rest of my life with, and I left Seattle with my daughter and moved back to North Carolina.

Ten years later, I met a man that I thought was a good man for me and I stayed with him for ten years. He died when I was fifty, and I would probably still be married to him today, had he not died. He was an excellent provider, and a wonderful man. During that decade of forty to fifty, I was with him and having a wonderful time teaching, traveling and enjoying my newfound freedom, because my daughter was now in college. It was also during this time that two other journeys in my life began. I became a grandmother, and then a caretaker to my mother who was stricken with Alzheimer's disease. I had all of these different roles I was playing, and there was not a lot of time to get caught up with Minnie, and what my lot was in life. I had too much to do.

From the time I was little, my mother always taught all of her children that we were God's favorites. I always believed I was very special to God, and knew that He would never leave me. He's never let me down.

When my husband died, I was fortunate to be able to date once again. I didn't feel guilty, because my husband was dead, and I needed to continue living and enjoying my life. I went out with lots of wonderful men, and some are still my friends to this very day. Since then, I met my new husband and we married, and life has been good.

"GET IN FRONT OF THE MIRROR, STRIP YOURSELVES NAKED, LOOK AT YOUR ROLLS AND ANY OTHER IMPERFECTIONS YOU FEEL YOU MIGHT HAVE, AND LOVE THEM ALL."

When I look back over who I was years ago, and who I am today, I realize that life's been a journey about finding myself. It took me until I reached my forties to actually understand the real Minnie. Even at sixty, I continue to learn a little bit more about me everyday. It's a journey of self-actualization, and you never, ever, fully reach the pinnacle.

My husband Ray and I have been married for almost four years, and we share such a wonderful connection that it feels like we've been married for twenty. We are, in fact, soul mates. He is my best friend, and we have wonderful times together and understand one another, even though he is seven years younger than me.

Now that I know who I am, I don't have to do anything I don't want to do. In your twenties, you allow people to help define you, letting them tell you what clothes to wear and even how to style your hair. I am marching to my own beat now, and living my own life. I say what I feel, and although I'm respectful to others, I'm not here to please anymore. I'm on this journey for myself, and that is true self-definition.

Now look ladies, you're going to get fat around your middle. Your breasts are going to sag a little, because gravity is taking over. That's part of aging. So what do we do? Well, if you don't exercise as much, maybe you're going to need something to support and help lift everything up. I don't mind shapers and foundations. I don't mind getting a little help where help is needed. Personally, I wouldn't go as far as having cosmetic surgery, but there are some who feel surgery is the right choice for them. At times, I'm going to deny myself some things that might not be good for me. Yes, I would love to eat key lime pie, Dunkin' Donuts, and yeast rolls everyday. But I know if I ate like that, I would blow up, just like the yeast in the rolls. So I have to temper myself and say, *"No, I won't do that."* I'm eating Special K or oatmeal in the morning, as opposed to bacon, eggs, sausage, grits and fried apples. I exercise and walk two miles a day, and often get on my stationary bike and watch TV while I ride. I'm running with my grandchildren, doing water aerobics, and dancing Zumba. Yes, sometimes it hurts, but I'm doing those things because I want to live a long and healthy life.

It's not been without its challenges. Things happen as you age, but that's okay! I've had surgery to remove a giant cell tumor from my leg. Some days I don't feel well, and on those days, if I don't feel like running, riding, dancing, or swimming—I don't do it. When I want to eat pancakes, I eat pancakes, but I don't eat them every day.

Les Brown says, *"Die empty."* That's what I'm looking forward to. When I am eighty-five, you can find me at the football games. I will be wearing tights and cowboy boots, sequins, and lipstick. I'm looking forward to being fabulous at every point in my life.

Women, love yourselves unconditionally. Get in front of the mirror, strip yourselves naked, look at your rolls and any other imperfections you feel you might have, and love them all. If you're losing your hair, go out and buy you some. If you're not happy with your teeth, go see a dentist. Need to lose weight, gain weight, or build your self-esteem? It's all within you to do. You have got to love the person that God created in His image and in His likeness, and you have got to love her more than you love anybody else.

WHAT GOLDEN NUGGETS DID YOU GET FROM THIS TREASURE CHEST OF WISDOM?

STRAIGHT TALK AND MEN'S THOUGHTS ON 40+ AND FABULOUS WOMEN

One of the biggest mistakes we make ladies, is consulting with each other about what goes on inside a man's head. When I was in high school, I had a really good guy friend who gave me some quick but valuable insight into the male psyche. He told me no matter what guys say they want you to do; and no matter how hard they plead with you to do it, deep down inside, what they really want...is a girl who won't. Yep, they can be difficult creatures to understand. Likewise, they wake up every-day, every bit as confused about us as we are about them. The old saying is true, *"It takes one to know one."* So when it came to *40+ and Fabulous*, I went straight to the source. I asked men of all ages to share what they found most alluring about women over forty. Ladies, the responses took my breath away and a couple even caused warning bells to go off in my head. The men you are about to meet did not hold back. They made me laugh, cry, and celebrate the greatness that is me, all over again!

I hope you will appreciate their candor as much as I did.

FRANK

Illinois

Age 46

I have always had an amazing relationship with my wife, RuthAnn. Let me give you just a bit of history.

When we first met, RuthAnn was 37 and I was 33. We had both been married two times prior to meeting, and were not looking for another marriage, but we were drawn together by something.

For me, that something was that RuthAnn was not only older than my previous wife, but was so very much more centered and independent. She knew what she wanted and was able to go after it with a determination that was inspiring. It seems like the moment she turned 40, the centeredness and determination increased exponentially. It drew her to me, and we got married. RuthAnn is now 50, and her personality and world view, are even more appealing to me now. Yes, it does truly happen that couples can become even happier after spending many years together.

I tell you this, because the very things that drew me to RuthAnn, are the things I find interesting, appealing, attractive, and exciting in women over forty. In my estimation, women over 40 have a spirit about them that is alluring. They are able to articulate what they want, need and desire in such a meaningful and attractive way. Let me say it straight out, it's sexy!

My dad used to kid my mom by saying that he was going to trade her in for "two twenties." Thank God he was just kidding. Over 40 and beautiful for me!

DAVE

Southern California
Age 32

I am a true "Cougar" lover.

They know what they want and are not afraid to go after it.

They demand things their own way because they know they are worth it. They hold you up to a higher standard, and that makes you a better person.

Sexually, they are generally well-studied and very open-minded.

PABLO

Texas
Age 61

I am an internationally recognized artist, known primarily for my drawings and sculptures of dancers. I have been featured in books, magazines, newspapers, radio, TV, and film. Currently, I live and work with my wife, Beverly, on our historic 1856 ranch north of Austin, Texas. Before serving as my full-time muse and business manager, Beverly was a model. She later went into sales and marketing for Diane von Furstenberg, Revlon, and Ralph Lauren. You can see my work at www.pablosolomon.com

As an artist, I work with some of the most beautiful women on earth. Although I am older than my wife, we have spent 34 wonderful years together. She has always been beautiful and is the love of my life. Even as she ages, she becomes more beautiful to me. Her figure is much fuller now, having gone from a near B, to a full D, and it all happened naturally. Yet she has maintained an hour glass shape and is very fit, due to yoga, biking, hiking and weights. From years of modeling, she knows how to put emotion into a pose.

And she is not alone. I have worked with several models for years, and as they all continue to age, they project a certain kind of wisdom in their sensuality. In fact, a short film that was run on HBO, featured my work with a model that at the time was in her late 40s. Younger women certainly have the fabulous bodies, but often do not have the passion or the confidence to model in a sensual manner. I find the same to be true in life. Women that have lived, learned, and experienced life, project confidence and sensuality. Often, younger women can project innocence which is grand, but just do not have that certain "something" that an older woman can project.

The older I get, the more I appreciate women who radiate a special beauty and passion that can only come from a lifetime of being a woman.

FRANK

Texas
Age 57

I find a mature woman who has experienced life appealing. She has a brain, is far more attractive than some cute young thing that only has the pneumatic physicality of youth, and/or expensive cosmetic surgery as her main attributes. Yes, believe it or not, there are men out here who do not buy into the "Barbi-esque Hollywood" stereotypes!

Give me a woman who can carry on an intelligent conversation, who has been somewhere besides the state next door, who has a broader frame of reference than whatever happens to be the topic du jour on "Oprah" or "Dr. Phil," and who has lived long enough to know that the brain is the most important erogenous zone of all. I love the smile lines next to a woman's eyes and mouth—they prove she can laugh—and I find an intelligent woman with a sense of humor incredibly sexy. And let's be honest, no matter how fantastic the sex in a relationship may be, at some point you have to get out of bed—and that is when I appreciate a woman who can communicate with wit and the special frame of reference that one only gains after years of living. I'm as appreciative as the next man of a well-toned physique...but it is truly hard to build a relationship on nothing more dynamic than ripped abs! Give me a woman who is truly comfortable in her own skin, who has lived and laughed and loved – and perhaps lost—but who understands that being well-rounded has nothing to do with saline or silicon!

I would not go back to being nineteen (or twenty-two, or even thirty-two) again! Even if I could—I value the lessons that life has taught me over the past fifty-seven years far too much—so why in the world would I want to try and pursue a relationship with a woman who cannot possibly relate to where I now am in my life?

And, do not think for a moment that I am some doddering old curmudgeon, bitterly watching life pass me by from the depths of my sofa! I lift weights, run, cycle, scuba dive, hike, sail, practice Tae kwon Do (2nd degree Black Belt), write Haiku, enjoy preparing and cooking oriental or southern cuisine, autocross my new Mini Cooper S, rebuild, restore and race classic British sports cars, and will travel for parts unknown at the drop of a hat! I read everything from Asimov to Zane Grey, and my generation invented rock music in all its iterations – metal, punk, soft, you name it - so a heavy back-beat and some righteous riffin' on the bridge, don't turn me off!!

I deeply love a woman who is exactly my age, and the main reason that I do love her is because she gets it—on so many different levels, SHE GETS IT—whether I'm talking about food and wine, theatre, politics, societal issues, sailing in the Carribean, or the nasty hook in turn five at Virginia International Raceway—she is articulate, opinionated, learned, dynamic, and experienced—I would not trade one moment with her for an entire night of wild excess with the most gorgeous, synthetically enhanced, pouting, pampered, over-coiffed, and ridiculously heavily made-up twenty-something waif-model icon of all that our youth-besotted society holds so dear. She has her own style, her own special take on the world around her, and she understands fashion without being a slave to the newest, latest, you-have-to-have-this–or-you're-not-cool momentary craze. She is mature without being too staid, she is experienced without being jaded, and she has weathered hard times in her life without becoming bitter, or overly cynical. She is, indeed, an "older woman" by society's ludicrously skewed standards—AND SHE ROCKS!!!

JIMMY

California

Age 33

I am an artist, I'm 33 years old and I have a great fondness for older women.

I spent the age of 28 to 31 as a single man, living in San Diego, CA. It was a transformative time for me, where I learned a great deal about myself and women. It was definitely a fun time as well. During those three years, I dated women ranging in age from 23 - 44, but most often it encompassed women in their early thirties - women closer to my age.

As those three years progressed, it was older women I was drawn to more and more. I gravitated to their maturity, straightforwardness, their greater volume of life experiences and the wisdom and perspectives that resulted from them. They seemed to have made it through their thirties, and now had a much clearer picture of what they wanted out of life. They played fewer games, and were confident in their sexuality. It was that developed inner clarity and their aggregate of experience, that enhanced their beauty for me. In my eyes, age had brought a patient elegance to them, and that was definitely a turn on.

Another big part of the equation for me was children. Most often kids were something a woman in her forties had already done, or had no intention of doing. Thus, my lack of desire to have kids of my own created no conflict. This was definitely an issue for the majority of women I dated that were in their early thirties, and while women in their twenties think about the 'kid thing' less, it is only a matter of time before it becomes a bridge that has to be crossed with them as well.

My girlfriend Annie, who is a certified dating and relationship coach and a yoga instructor, is the last person I dated in San Diego. She is 45 years old, and is the most amazing woman I have ever met. We have been together for a year and a half now. Three months after we first met, she asked me to move abroad with her. Five months after that, we did. Today, we currently live in Buenos Aires, Argentina. One day we will make our way back to California, but for now our adventures continue here.

ERIC

California
Age 36

I can heartily endorse older women. Although it was a few years ago, and I've since married someone else, Cecily was easily one of the most fun, intelligent, and gorgeous women I've ever dated. She was a nurse, and an officer in the U.S. Army Reserve. I sometimes think of her, and wish I had kept in touch.

I was just 22 years old, recently back from Basic and Advanced Training with the Army, attending my first Annual Training event with my Utah-based Army Reserve Unit near Dublin, California. I had grown up in the Sonoma County Wine Country, so I got *"voluntold"* to escort four of the nurses on a tour of the area on one of our off days. One of the nurses was Cecily, and we hit it off. She was 42, but seemed very easy to talk to, and we had a great time driving through Sonoma County together.

After getting back to Utah, she and I were among the last people to leave the area, and she noticed that I rode a motorcycle, and asked if we could go for a ride sometime. That turned into a dinner date, and I met her parents then—who also drove up on a motorcycle. I knew then that we would get along pretty well. We dated for a few weeks, and then mission requirements came up that separated us for awhile. After that, I guess we just lost touch.

JEFFREY

Washington, DC
Age 34

Out of the more than 300 women I have dated (yes, most of them were very short-term relationships!), I would estimate that 50% were 5-10 years my senior, and about 15% were in their forties at the time we dated. In my twenties, I even went out with a couple of women who were in their 50's. I love older women!

Older women are smarter, sexier, more elegant, well-traveled, interesting, self-aware, and confident (and what is more sexy than confidence?). They are more graceful, grace-giving, and appreciative of attention. They are also more content in their current phase of life, not adding unnecessary commitment pressure to dating scenarios. In many cases, they are in no hurry to inch closer towards another potentially painful breakup or divorce, and thus, often prefer more casual dating.

When paired with a commitment-phobic younger man, that woman has better odds of a successful (although often short-term), fun, and fulfilling dating experience, without the constraints often applied by younger, more insecure, needy mates. Both parties have expectations that are easier to meet; and the disappointment is significantly lesser if they are not met. Should the relationship head south, the odds are greater that some degree of friendship can be preserved, without the typical baggage that accompanies younger break-ups. Since these women are more interesting, engaging, and lower maintenance, those friendships are more worthy of preservation.

Additionally, I find that older women are more understanding and forgiving of a younger man's propensity towards promiscuous dating patterns, in the absence of a serious commitment, of course. The women may very well have similar desires. But, do older women really want a serious, longer-term relationship with a younger man? Not likely, unless we are already bald, chubby, and rich! So, with minimal pain and awkward excuses, these relationships naturally fizzle out, and then true friendships can be fostered. To sum it up, I offer a quote that I coined years ago that partially describes why I date older women: *'because it ends itself.'*

BRUCE

Georgia
Age: 65

I am a singer/songwriter. About a year ago I was taking my mother-in-law to lunch, and the hostess sat us beside a table full of women in red hats. It was my introduction to the *Red Hat Society*. They were having quite a time. The experience spawned an idea for a song. I wrote and recorded it within a few weeks, and it is one of my most requested songs, particularly at private gigs for women having birthdays.

The song is titled *Woman of a Certain Age*, and I would be honored to have it included in your book.

Hearts, she broke a few
And her own a time or two
Some scars you see
Some don't show
Fools, she suffered some,
Almost nothing she hasn't done
She's got secrets we'll never know

40+ AND FABULOUS

She sorted it out and tucked it away
Knew she'd need it one of these days
Every year she slowly turns the page
She's a woman of a certain age

Won't lead you on, won't play that game,
Savors the pleasures, accepts the pain
Now that she looks at life with a clearer view,
Wants quiet talk and expensive wine,
She gets it right because she gives it time
Admit it boy, you're one of the lucky few

Oh, the choices she could have made
All the others she knew
And the roads she did not take
Because of you

She sorted it out and tucked it away
Knew she'd need it one of these days
Now every year she slowly turns the page
She's a woman of a certain age

DERRICK

Georgia
Age 38

This story is called W.O.E.: How my wife saved my life.

A few years ago, my life hit rock bottom. My ex-wife and the mother of my children, said she no longer wanted to be with me. I wanted to start over, so I moved from Alabama to Georgia.

Mind you, I had limited money, no job, and no place to stay. A childhood friend said I could sleep on his floor until I could get back on my feet.

It was my first Friday night in a new city, and my friend asked me to go out and dance. I refused at first, but I later realized I needed to get out for some air.

I asked an attractive young lady named Kim to dance, and we grooved until the lights came on and it was time for us to go. We exchanged numbers. I never expected to meet someone so nice and so quickly. The even crazier thing is that she lived 90 miles away.

I was thinking about how my life had changed and I said, "Woe." I looked in the Bible and I found the word woe. I also wanted to see how the dictionary defined it. Woe means trials or tribulations. In life, a woe to you might be a job loss, and to someone else, it might be a broken relationship.

One day, I was thinking about how I could reinvent my life, and I wrote down the word "woe" on a piece of paper.

As the document spoke to me, it revealed that woe now meant WOE as in Word of Encouragement. From there I received this slogan. *"Before you leave work or go to sleep tonight, give someone a WOE, a Word of Encouragement."*

I shared my concept of WOE with Kim, and we decided that before we ended our conversation each night, someone had to give a WOE. We have been together for six years, since our first dance.

She has been the light of my life. Kim is 43, and she helped me go from woe to WOE!

RYAN

New York
Age 26

I'm a writer of a sex and relationship column, and have had experiences with older women. This topic is a personal favorite of mine. I've actually tossed around the idea of writing a book, based upon my experiences, specifically, those of cougars and other cougar bait.

Through conversation and physical experience, I've learned that older women have a sense of maturity that runs far beyond their age. By the age of 40, women are established, secure in both their career and in their life. It's a known fact that women reach their sexual peak in their 30's or 40's. This time in a woman's life provides a sense of evident empowerment. I've seen it on all levels. Unfortunately, the older men in their lives are well beyond their sexual peak, and can't satisfy these highly charged women. By this time, a lot of women who live in passionless, lustless marriages have a yearning to be satisfied, both sexually and sensually. This desire is not just about sex; it's about attention. It's about someone else focusing on her needs.

I've spoken to many older women, other than those that I've been with, and they all state the same general feelings. Their husbands don't show them enough attention, either because they are sexually disconnected from the relationship, or are too tired to care. Nonetheless, a woman's mind will run wild and she will fantasize about experiencing these feelings. The question isn't whether or not she'll visualize; it's whether or not she'll act on these thoughts. This known piece of information is one key ingredient that sparks the curiosity of any male in their 20's, like me.

Personally, if I know an older single woman, a divorcee, or even a married woman isn't happy or stimulated in their personal life, that's a turn on. I don't enjoy their misfortunes; rather look at their needs as an opportunity for me to fulfill them.

I've been with two divorced women that admitted they got married too young, were never truly happy with their sex lives and felt that as newly single women, it was time to get what they wanted. I love the fact that an older woman looks at me to fill a void. It's knowing that I can fulfill the needs her husband couldn't, that is such an intoxicating feeling. Older women are willing to try new things and explore long time curiosities that have lingered throughout monotonous relationships. I enjoy giving older women the attention, both on a sensual and sexual level, they haven't gotten in over a decade. Providing these types of experiences are enjoyable for me and that, within itself, is pleasurable.

On a narcissistic level, I love how older women look at me and my body with craving intensity. The middle-aged men in their lives are fat, hairy and couldn't care less about their appearance. I, on the other hand, stay active, work out and take pride in how I look. A woman enjoys being wanted by an attractive man with energy and attention to give. Women feel young when they interact with a younger guy; they feel desired; and who doesn't want to be desired?

But in the end, older women are awesome because they're doing what they want to do. It's not about making the man happy. It's about wanting something and going out and getting it. Luckily for me, they can get it from the twenty-something. And for that, I'm turned on.

TREY

Texas
Age 23

Since I have been a physically mature adult, I have been able to appreciate older women. The most appealing and attractive trait I have found in most older women is that they know deep down who they are, what they want, and their purpose on this earth, more so than younger women. This trait seems to be inborn in some, while most have developed it over years of raising children, or working many different jobs until they found one that they are passionate on a deep level about. Another trait of older women that is very attractive, is the fact that they have experienced more life than I have, and are more mentally mature than younger women. I notice that because of this, I am able to have much more interesting conversations with them about a wide variety of topics, usually gaining views and insights that I had previously never thought of, or heard before. What older women lack in physical beauty and surface attraction for me, can easily be made up if they possess the aforementioned traits that stay for life; unlike physical beauty which fades with time.

GEORGE

Mississippi
Age 35

I met my wife Susie when I was only 19 and she was 38. We are a little over 19 years apart in age, but closer than anyone could ever be. This November, we will have been together for 16 years, and it has just been wonderful, and I would not trade it for all the sexy, beautiful young women out there today. I believe that God brought us together, because our relationship is just that special. Susie is so interesting and always up to something, kinda' like *I Love Lucy*. She is full of life and funny; always finding humor in a situation. The appealing part is that she doesn't need to play games and talk about herself all of the time. She loves to do things for me; cook, take care of me when I am sick, wash my clothes and teach me things that she already knows, just by living life a little more than me. I love older women. They are smart, sexy, and they know how to treat a man and appreciate us for who we are, just men. Older ladies are so sweet to me, they just love the attention I give them, and I love the attention they show me. I love Susie with all my heart, and I feel like the luckiest person in the world to have her by my side. I really feel sorry for these guys who have to have a young trophy girl by their side, there is so much more to a real relationship and love, and I am so glad I know it.

DARRELL

North Carolina
Age 42

Well, let me tell you from the jump! 40 is AWESOME! Now understand, this is coming from a brother that thought he had it going on throughout his 20's and 30's. I have always been very confident in my ability to live life to the fullest. I was never the best at one thing, but felt that I was pretty darn good at a lot of things. So while marching around the campus of North Carolina A&T State University, I was enjoying my youth. I never spent much time thinking about getting old and how I would accept it. Living for the moment was my thing. At that time, if I would have spent five minutes on thinking about how life would be at forty, I would pretty much have assumed that life would be dull. I would have thought about what my father did at the age of forty. A life of complacency and routine would have been the vision. I would have pictured me having a wilting body, and my wife walking around in a house robe at 7:00 p.m., and going to bed by 9:00. My life is as far from this as the sun is from the earth. What made the difference? The woman in my life!

My college sweetheart caught my eye early on, during my young college life. We were both the same age, even though she entered college a year after me. Together, we were always referred to by others as being a very cute couple. I would have to say, even back then, I thought that those comments were merely in order to make me feel good, because at the tender age of 18, I recognized that she was the better half of the couple.

We continued dating for six years and finally married. After being married now for eighteen years, and having two children together, this woman is still like the seventeen year old that I met twenty five years ago. The day she turned that BEAUTIFUL age of 40, was physically noticed by no one. My wife weighed 115 pounds when we married in 1991, is today still holding tight at 117 pounds, and it's hard to believe that we are parents to a 15 and 20 year old. Even to this day, people still cannot believe she's 42 years of age. The first thing that comes out of someone's mouth is, *"Get the hell out of here!"* *"Yep, she's forty,"* is always my response.

I feel blessed to walk the streets with this woman on my arm, showing her off as my better half. I'm not ashamed to say that she compliments me in every way. In order to not feel this relationship is one sided, I felt it was only fair that I work to improve my looks and keep my body and health up to par. For years I have spent 5 days a week, going through a tough regimented work out at the gym. I have put my body through tough times to stay in the best of shape. I would have to say, it has paid off. So in order to compliment what my wife was contributing in just sheer beauty as we aged, I gave her a little to feel proud of as well. I try to keep a well defined physique, naturally – no drugs or supplements. I often joke, that if you were to line up 20, twenty-five year olds and judge us by appearance, if I'm not number one, I would definitely be in the top three! This is just a joke, of course, but spoken as a confident forty plus man. We both now represent the 40 plus crowd in a very positive way.

DARRELL

Three years ago, I had shirts made that read, *"40+ and Awesome, We're Bringing Sexy Back."* I started by selling the shirts and used my wife as a walking billboard. They started selling like hot cakes. I then began handing out the shirts, because I wanted everyone to notice just how awesome the forty plus crowd really was.

At the age of forty-two, when most people think you would be on the down side of the game of life, I am here to tell you that my wife has tilted the scale the other way. We are getting more enjoyment out of life now, than ever before. Fortunately for us, our kids are much older in age than most of our friend's children. With one child in college and one midway through high school, it allows us the freedom to do more together and enjoy what life has to offer. We travel more now, and attend livelier functions. Our date night starts on Thursday night, and begins our weekend of fun. Finding us at a lounge or dining out at a hot spot in town, has become our norm. I love to see her dress up for our outings. If she wears classy attire and looks strikingly sexy, it doesn't bother me, in fact, I feel even prouder to have her as my wife. I have grown to accept the stares men give my wife. That only enhances my gratitude of what she has to offer.

Our sex life has gotten hotter as we've grown older. The assumption of banging like rabbits at a young age and needing supplemental support to keep the fire going as we age, is just that -- an assumption. There has been a reverse drive in sexual desire. We are more sexually active now than we were 15 years ago. I'm not saying that we are wrinkling the sheets every night, but we weren't doing that at twenty-five. There has been a change in command in the bedroom. I used to take charge and call the plays, and I now follow the orders and run the play as called by her.

I know it doesn't end with just MY wife. I hear it across the board from men with women over 40. The names are changed, but the stories remain the same. Women over forty are a new breed!

So, I'm here to tell you that, regardless of what they say, forty is NOT the new thirty, because thirty NEVER rocked like this!

THE "AH-HAH" COLLECTION

DONNA HILL

Age: 58

Volunteer Publicist, Performing Arts Division,

National Federation of the Blind

Whenever you are doing what is in your heart to do, your self-esteem will always reap the benefits.

Obviously, as a blind person, I'm not looking at whether you're physically attractive, if you're in style, or how well your hair or makeup is done. Those concepts of beauty are totally foreign to me. A woman's beauty has to do with how she engages the world. When a person reaches out into the world, present and in the moment, filled with honesty and good intentions, that is what I see as being extremely attractive.

ELIZABETH HARPER

Age: 48

Author, Psychic Artist, Color Energy Healer

If I were a light, I was on the dimmer setting before I turned forty. Now that I'm in my forties, I am on full power and shining my light for all to see.

My mother always said, *"What a caterpillar calls death, the master calls a butterfly."* I died at thirty-nine and became a butterfly at forty.

SUSAN JASIN

Age: 62

Owner of Fleur d'Lis School of Baking & Pastry

I'm a living example that it's never too late to follow your heart. I was a psychologist, and later, became the GM of a manufacturing company. After I retired, I lived my dream by attending pastry school for a year. At age 59, I opened my own wholesale pastry business; serving caterers, restaurants and hotels. Now, at the age of 62, I am also running my own baking school.

What you will discover is that life actually begins at 50.

The perfect body no longer has to do with cellulite, or proportion between measurements and various parts. A perfect body is when everything works and nothing hurts.

KIMBERLY HAYES TAYLOR

Age: 48

Author, Speaker, Freelance Journalist, Pulitzer Prize Nominee

I don't have any reservations about making bold changes at this point in my life.

I look better with age; much better now than I did when I was twenty or twenty five, and if you don't believe me, I can show you pictures.

Needing people's opinions about me and what I should be doing is a thing of the past.

I'm having a love affair with myself. And I've learned that no matter what I do or what mistakes I make, I'm still okay.

JAYNE FERRER

Age: 53

Author and Word Woman

There's something I tell my friends who are turning forty and that is, *"It's the most freeing thing that will ever happen you."*

I love that wisdom and security and confidence you see in older women.

One of the things that really separate the sheep from the lambs, is the ability to face challenges with a positive outlook. You can either let life overwhelm you and drag you down, or you can look it boldly in the face and say, *"Okay, what's the best way to deal with this?"*

I don't understand why everyone thinks menopause is such a bad thing. The morning I turned fifty, I thought, *"Okay, bring it on, this is the day!"* I'm ready for my money to go to something else besides feminine hygiene supplies!

Melody Brooke

Age: 53

Author *"Oh Wow! This Changes Everything"*
Co-Author *"Oh Wow! This is Great Sex!"*

The truth is, we know ourselves better over forty. We know what we need, we know what we like, and we're not afraid to ask for what is good for us.

Audretta Hall

Age: 44

Relationship Marketing Expert

I consider forty to be a right of passage. The children of Israel wandered around the desert for forty years until they figured out exactly where they needed to be.

Before forty, my mom said I was, *"running through the jungle, whooping lions with a switch."* But the closer I got to forty, the more clarity I had about things. I hadn't yet put all the pieces together, but I was beginning to feel a sense of divine urgency to have my calling complete.

I feel responsible to let women in their twenties and thirties know, *"Hey, you're going to get here, but there are some things you're going to have to go through first."*

I refer to my twenties as my crying years. I cried when I was happy, when I was sad, and even when nothing was going on. Now that I'm in my forties, the stuff I used to cry about, I don't even blink an eye at!

I plan to be the finest 90 year old they'll ever bury. So, I do the things I need to do, in order to take good care of myself from the inside out.

Paris Tompkins

Age: 66

Owner, The Oodles Company

In my younger years, I just did things as they presented themselves. I handled things as they came along only I didn't have as much control. I didn't feel I had choices, and in particular, I didn't feel I could say *"no."* I have since been empowered by maturing.

ARDY SKINNER

Age: 44

Author, The Lavish Cheapskate

When I was young, I was ignorant about the way a lot of things worked in the world. As we go through major changes in our life, the ignorance slowly dissipates.

I believe the rock bottoms and the dark places in my life have been a great opportunity, not only to grow personally, but to pay it forward to my daughter; to pass it on to other women, to show them I am a human being experiencing this journey, and it's okay. Not only is it okay, but you can actually use those rock bottom experiences to catapult you into something magnificent.

AFTERWORD

Socrates said, *"Do what makes your heart leap."* Writing this book for you has made my heart leap.

At forty plus, these women are having the best time of their lives. They have let go of the past, and have a clear vision of the future. They are enjoying newfound freedom; freedom from worrying about what others think, freedom from rearing children, freedom from pads and tampons, and freedom to explore new directions. And even with grey hair, wrinkles, love handles and butt rolls - many find themselves more physically attractive now than ever before.

Some exercise, some don't. Some are for surgical enhancement; some are content with letting nature take her course. Some love being married, and some marvel in their singleness. Some are super ambitious, and some are happy just where they are.

At first glance, it may appear that these women contradict what being forty plus and fabulous is all about. But, there is no contradiction here at all. Because what they are saying is you can, at last, listen to your own voice. Forty plus and fabulous is about doing it your way, finding satisfaction, self-acceptance and love.

When I look at my nine year old niece, Barrington, who is the apple of my eye, how I long to be able to inject her with all I have learned; protecting her from the pain of disappointment and the sadness of heartbreak. It's not meant to be that way. Just as I thought two living cheaper than one was a recipe for a successful marriage, she will have to have her own unique experiences that shape her life. After all, only the wisdom that comes with time and experience can truly make one Forty Plus and Fabulous. What we must do is continue to break down the negative stereotypes of aging and give women positive and powerful images of women at midlife and beyond.

Women who have learned from life's mistakes, embraced self-for-giveness, let go of things that could not be changed, and are now able to move forward – fierce, focused and full of life!

"We don't receive wisdom; we must discover it for ourselves after a journey that no one can take for us or spare us."
—Marcel Proust (1871-1922)

ABOUT THE AUTHOR

SONDRA WRIGHT is a graduate of North Carolina Agricultural and Technical State University with a Bachelor's Degree in Psychology and a Master's Degree in Counseling and Human Services with a concentration in Human Resources. A member of Alpha Kappa Alpha Sorority, Inc., she is active in a variety of community projects involved in the needs of the elderly, childhood literacy, and the socio-economic advancement of women and children.

Her passion is inspiring the breakthrough and change necessary for women to reach their maximum potential. She lives in Greensboro, North Carolina with her husband, John. *40+ and Fabulous* is her debut book.

Connect with Sondra at facebook.com/40plusandfabulous and twitter.com/fortyplusandfab.

CONTRIBUTORS' DIRECTORY

In Order of Appearance

Tonoa Bond
The Audacity Expert™
www.TonoaBond.com
www.TheBondInstitute.com

Jane Ganahl
Journalist, Author, Consultant, Editor and Community Organizer
www.janeganahl.com

Darlene Bauer
Retired English Teacher, President of Barthur House Publishing
www.hostorhostage.com

Eileen Fulton
Television and Broadway Actress
Lisa Miller, CBS *As The World Turns*
www.EileenFultonOnline.com

Elline Surianello
The Leading Authority on Women's Hair Thinning and Hair Loss
www.lemetric.com

Norma Hollis
America's Leading Authentic Voice Doctor
www.normahollisspeaks.com

Terry Kohl
President of Incredible Things, Media Management Marketing
www.terrykohl.com

Dr. Johnetta B. Cole
President Emerita, Bennett College for Women and Spelman College
Director of the National Museum of African Art
www.jbcinstitute.org

Kim Cameron
Singer and Songwriter, Side FX Band
www.kimcameronmusic.com

195

Tanya Hutchinson
Mrs. California International 2005
Winner, Reality TV's She's Got the Look
Founder, Phenomenal Women, Inc
www.phenomenalwomeninc.org

Roselle Wilson
Boutique Owner
www.ladymarians.com

Kim Harris
Training and Development Consultant
www.possibility-thinker.com

Brenda Pollard
Educator, Memphis City Schools
Co-author, *Literacy Workstations* Handbook
State and National Educational Presenter on Teaching At-Risk Youth

Alice "A J" Johnson
Jamali Fashion & Accessories
935 Chattahoochee Ave NW
Atlanta, GA 30318
www.jamalifashion.com

Nancy Cranbourne
Choreographer and Director, 40 Women Over 40
www.nancycranbourne.com
www.40womenover40.com

Yana Berlin
Founder of Fabulously40.com
www.fabulously40.com

Eva LaRue
Former Miss California Empire, Model and Actress
Dr. Maria Santos Grey, *All My Children,* Detective Natalia Boa Vista, *CSI: Miami*
www.evalarue.com

Sue Taylor
Legal Administration
www.suething.wordpress.com

Joanne and Barbara
Cartoonists and Founders of Perrie Meno-Pudge
www.perriemenopudge.com

CONTRIBUTORS' DIRECTORY

Connie Vasquez
Attorney and Founder of Vintage Awesome
vintageawesome.wordpress.com
lostmymomburiedmymind.blogspot.com

Loretta Petit
Radio Personality and Ordained Elder
www.lorettapetit.com

Catherine Hickland
Singer, Actress and Stage Hypnotist
www.catherinehickland.com

Acharya Sri Khadi Madama
World Renowned Registered Yoga Teacher
www.yourstrulyyogatv.vpweb.com

Tina Stull
NHRA Professional Drag Racer
www.tinastullracing.com

Judie Bucholz
Regional Dean, Onsite Programs, Strayer University

Yolanda Carr
Doctoral Student and Grants Coordinator, University of Arkansas

Andrea Vanessa Wright
Co-founder Warriors, Inc.
www.warriorsincnc.org

Minnie Forte-Brown
Professor, North Carolina Central University
Chairwoman, Durham Public Schools Board of Education
Appointee, North Carolina Council of Women

Donna Hill
Volunteer Publicist, Performing Arts Division, National Federation of the Blind

Elizabeth Harper
Psychic Artist, Color Energy Healer, Spiritual Guide and Teacher
www.sealedwithlove.com

Susan Jasin
Fleur d' Lis School of Baking & Pastry
www.fleurdliscandy.com

Kimberly Hayes Taylor
Intuitive Writer, Speaker and Coach
www.kimberlyhayestaylor.com

Jayne Ferrer
Writer, Poet and Speaker
www.jaynejaudonferrer.com

Melody Brooke
Marriage Therapist and Counselor
www.awakenedheartproductions.com

Audretta Hall
Relationship Marketing Expert
www.support4yourdreams.com

Paris Tompkins
Creator of Children's Storybooks and Black Ragdolls
www.thefirsttrip.com

Ardy Skinner
Direct Response Marketer
www.lavishcheapskate.com

WE INVITE YOU TO CONTINUE YOUR 40+ AND FABULOUS JOURNEY AT OUR WEBSITE.

www.40plusandfabulous.com

- Share how you feel about *40+ and Fabulous* and read what others are saying

- Share your golden nuggets of wisdom and discuss ah-ha's with other readers at the *40+ and Fabulous* blog

- Request notification of upcoming events

- Communicate with Sondra

- Purchase additional copies of *40+ and Fabulous*

- Request information on having Sondra speak at a *40+ and Fabulous* event for your group

CPSIA information can be obtained at www.ICGtesting.com
Printed in the USA
BVOW010441151012

302980BV00003B/2/P